Cambridge Elements ☰

Elements in the Global Middle Ages
edited by
Geraldine Heng
University of Texas at Austin
Susan Noakes
University of Minnesota Twin Cities

THE MARKET IN POETRY IN THE PERSIAN WORLD

Shahzad Bashir
Brown University

CAMBRIDGE
UNIVERSITY PRESS

University Printing House, Cambridge CB2 8BS, United Kingdom

One Liberty Plaza, 20th Floor, New York, NY 10006, USA

477 Williamstown Road, Port Melbourne, VIC 3207, Australia

314–321, 3rd Floor, Plot 3, Splendor Forum, Jasola District Centre,
New Delhi – 110025, India

103 Penang Road, #05–06/07, Visioncrest Commercial, Singapore 238467

Cambridge University Press is part of the University of Cambridge.

It furthers the University's mission by disseminating knowledge in the pursuit of
education, learning, and research at the highest international levels of excellence.

www.cambridge.org
Information on this title: www.cambridge.org/9781108948647
DOI: 10.1017/9781108953016

© Shahzad Bashir 2021

First published 2021

A catalogue record for this publication is available from the British Library.

ISBN 978-1-108-94864-7 Paperback
ISSN 2632-3427 (online)
ISSN 2632-3419 (print)

Cambridge University Press has no responsibility for the persistence or accuracy of
URLs for external or third-party internet websites referred to in this publication
and does not guarantee that any content on such websites is, or will remain,
accurate or appropriate.

The Market in Poetry in the Persian World

Elements in the Global Middle Ages

DOI: 10.1017/9781108953016
First published online: November 2021

Shahzad Bashir
Brown University

Author for correspondence: Shahzad Bashir, shahzad_bashir@brown.edu

Abstract: "Poetic speech is a pearl, connected to the king's ear." This statement gestures to words as objects of material value sought by those with power and resources. The author provides a sense for the texture of the Persian world by discussing what made poetry precious. By focusing on reports on poets' lives, they illuminate the social scene in which poetry was produced and consumed. The discussion elicits poetry's close connections to political and religious authority, economic exchange, and the articulation of gender. At the broadest level, the study substantiates the interdependency between cultural and material reproduction of society.

Keywords: Persian poetry, Iran, South Asia, Central Asia, Middle Ages

ISBNs: 9781108948647 (PB), 9781108953016 (OC)
ISSNs: 2632-3427 (online), 2632-3419 (print)

Contents

Introduction

The origins of this Element go back to a moment many years ago when I came across an image regarding poetry in Zayn Khān Khwāfi's (d. 1533) partial Persian translation of the memoirs of Bābor (d. 1530), the founder of the Mughal dynasty in India. Writing in Chaghatay Turkish, Bābor mentions that, on the way to India in December 1525, he got separated from his troops during a river excursion. Adrift on a raft, the company took to the familiar pastime of composing poetic responses. Bābor offered the following Persian verse by a contemporary poet as the muse:

> What is one to do with a beloved full of flirting.
> Wherever you are, what is one to do with anyone else.
> *(Bābor, 1995: 405)*

The scene in Bābor's memoir is evocative enough to have become the subject of a painting accompanying the text in a sumptuous manuscript produced in the late sixteenth century (see Figure 1). Khwāfi's translation of Bābor's memoir is adaptive rather than literal. His text refers to Bābor in the third person, transforming the original self-narrative into a report. Having mentioned the verse, he departs from the original to remark that Bābor's companions obeyed his command per the dictum, put into a hemistich, that a verse worthy of a king is a precious pearl. Their combined efforts were then comparable to elaborate jewelry dangling from the king's ear (Khwāfi, n.d.: 11a).

It struck me that comparing a pearl earring to a verse was especially apt as a means to understand poetic production as a market of goods and services in societies in the Middle Ages where Persian was an important literary medium. There is, first of all, the fact that the piece of jewelry and the pronounced verse intersect on the human ear. As objects denoting luxury and power, pearls were considered extremely valuable throughout Eurasia. Pearls were a paramount commodity involved in processes of mediation and exchange. Among rulers and other elites, pearls were acquired, displayed, gifted, stolen, and counterfeited as a part of political and economic activity. Pearls' value was a naturalized fact in this setting, creating the conditions that made them a form of fungible currency (Allsen, 2019). In societies where Persian mattered, circulation of poetry can be seen as analogous to the use of pearls. In the two cases, respectively, the worth of the material entity (a pearl) and the materialized product (a poetic utterance) reflected their enmeshment in political, economic, and aesthetic relations that permeated social imagination and experienced reality.

Figure 1 "Bābor Riding a Raft." From a copy of *Bābornāmeh*. Sixteenth century, India. Ink and pigments on remargined paper: 32 × 21 cm. The Walters Art Museum, Baltimore. W.596, Folio 17b.

Describing a poem made of verses as a string of pearls is a common metaphor in literary expression in Persian and associated traditions (Landau, 2015). My purpose here is to take the materiality implied in the metaphor seriously as a means to understanding social worlds. Here I understand materiality as an overarching abstraction denoting relationships between physical objects, verbal utterances, mental ideas and images, and corporeal movements that constitute the framework for lived experience (Miller, 2005). My proposition, in essence, is that, in the societies where it mattered, Persian poetry was valued so highly as to permeate human beings' senses of themselves and all that surrounded them in the form of a materialized cosmos.

Poetry was regarded as a prized form of language generated by people possessing a combination of innate ability and acquired skill. While versification was exceedingly widespread, poetic talent – evaluated based on parameters I will discuss – was a finite resource. This made accomplished poets valuable craftspeople. Moreover, collecting and maintaining poetry in memory or on paper was akin to gathering a treasury. For those with resources, this required cultivating another cadre of people, those who articulated standards, analyzed and judged the words, and produced historical records to commemorate the virtuosi.

Poetry was also a linguistic vehicle uniquely suited to transmit knowledge meant to circulate within a restricted group. As verbal signification not meant to be taken literally, poetic speech was amenable to coding and jargon. This made it a mainstay of literature among Sufis and others who espoused forms of esotericism. Similarly, poetry was essential to the allusion-filled communications of elite secretaries who ran bureaucracy and diplomacy. Given these characteristics, Persian poetry's footprint as a social matter affords us an especially rich view of life's complexity during the Middle Ages.

The Persian World

I should explain that the "Persian world," as mentioned in the title of this Element, signifies a spatiotemporal abstraction keyed to a literary language. I have deliberately chosen this as the arena I wish to represent rather than specifying the topic based on periodization affixed to calendars and regions (history of Asia, the Middle East, etc.). In theoretical work pertaining to history, problems involved in using geographical and temporal markers as the basis for delimiting topics are well known by now (e.g. Bashir, forthcoming 2022; Black, 2018; Tanaka, 2019). This pertains especially to terms such as "the Middle Ages," "medieval," "early modern," and so on that have bequeathed us ideologically inflected methodological and disciplinary exclusions. By displacing the matter to language use, I aim to contribute to the subversive intent of Global Middle Ages Elements. My objective is not to arrive at pristine new categories, untainted by problems. Rather, the usage is meant to spur appreciation for how categories inflect analyses toward particular ends.

My conceptualization invites seeing synchronic and diachronic connectivity in societies through the lens of a common language rather than maps, chronologies, and genealogies. In the course of my discussion, I do identify locations by names and provide Common Era dates in order to make the narrative legible in established vocabularies. However, I treat language use as the meta principle in order to highlight the autochthonous logic of my materials, in which connectivity is a matter of literary citation and not abstract chronology. Moreover, the choice can help us remain mindful of the fact that the cultural patterns I am describing are not the ruins of a dead past. Persian remains a major world language to this day. Especially in its modern institutionalized forms in Afghanistan, Iran, and Tajikistan, the poetic world I discuss is a crucial component of sociocultural inheritance for tens of millions in our contemporary world (Haeri, 2021; Najafian, 2018; Olszewska, 2015; Rubanovich, 2015; Schwartz, 2020; Van den Berg, 2004).

The phrase "Persian world" is a heuristic abstraction also because it can never be the sole descriptor for a society that existed in the past. My usage here is aligned with the notion that complex social settings are comprised of "divergent worldings constantly coming about through negotiations, enmeshments, crossings, and interruptions" (de la Cadena and Blaser, 2018: 6). Any given social situation always includes many worlds, tied to variant senses of time and space imbricated in subjectivities involved in social processes. It is important to keep in mind, then, that no society has ever existed in which Persian would be the only language of communication. From its ninth-century inception as the vernacular of peoples living in the Iranian plateau and Central Asia to today, Persian has always been a part of multilingual environments. On the literary side, this pertains to similar worlds of Arabic, Kurdish, various forms of Turkish, Hebrew, Pashto, Sanskrit, Braj Bhasha, Urdu-Hindi, Bangla, and so on. All these other worlds can be treated in a way similar to what I am attempting for Persian. My choice has to do with creating a limited topic rather than proclaiming Persian's superiority or greater significance.

For the spoken realm, Persian itself has a myriad of dialects, all utilized simultaneously with literary Persian and forms of other languages. In modern situations the world over, Persian coexists with major European languages such as English, French, German, and Italian. Amidst all this diversity, a focus on the world of formalized poetry in Persian is a choice meant to facilitate analysis rather than a descriptive claim about a specific society.

In some cases, the relationship between Persian and other languages involves transmission of literary patterns. This has led to the neologism "Persianate" from Persian, on the pattern of Italianate from Italian (Amanat and Ashraf, 2018; Green, 2019). I avoid this term for the reason that, to my mind, it can imply a presumption of hierarchy between Persian and other linguistic worlds. In parallel with the critique of "cosmopolitanism" as a category implying a built-in elitism, positing Persian as the lingua franca of a premodern "cosmopolis," anchored in a literary medium, can have the effect of rendering nonparticipants uncosmopolitan, and hence, lesser beings in terms of cultural sophistication (Mignolo, 2000). For my purposes, the adjective "Persian" has the same explanatory efficacy as "Persianate," while it also avoids signifying stratification in the process of discussing literary and cultural connectivity.

The Market

The invocation of a "market" in the title of this essay is a strategic reification to create an exploratory arena. This is akin to how we talk about the stock or commodity markets tied to goods and services, which go up or down, even though we know that these are not entities with agency but abstractions denoting a set of human relations. Through the market metaphor, I wish to highlight poetry's place in the overlap between metaphysics and materiality. As language, poetic expression is a product of the mind, tied to matters pertaining to ontology, cosmology, epistemology, and rhetoric. But the language is discernible only when it appears on paper, buildings, and other media. Put to speech via the human mouth, poetry becomes embodied, forming the basis for conversation, recitation, and rituals.

As a diversified and changing art form, poetry is an intangible but pervasive and highly valued discourse. When instantiated as a verse that is spoken or written, poetry is a tangible, materialized object, with exchange value accruing to those able to produce or reproduce it. Processes for creating and valuing poetry that I discuss in this Element hearken consistently to its double valuation as discourse and object. Concentrating on play pertaining to Persian poetry in the Middle Ages provides views into social dynamics at the broadest level.

In Persian literary history, social aspects of poetic production have been discussed predominantly through highlighting relationships between patrons and poets. By invoking the market, I wish to displace our understanding of poets' positioning as a matter of elite patronage alone. In my conceptualization, the market and patronage are interlocked social processes. When employed by royal figures or other elites, poets may certainly be described as one half of patronage relationships that formed the economic basis for the production of poetry. However, I see the dyadic relationship as a part of the wider market within which poets and their words circulated among patrons spread over a vast geography. Many significant poets were wealthy and socially advantaged to the point of not needing patronage. Poetry was a mainstay of cultural life among all classes. Because of these factors, a market comprised of the exchange of material goods and social capital is an especially useful framework with which to understand poetry as a social matter. The greater capacity of the market metaphor helps us see poetic production as a part of socioeconomic relations that went beyond patron–poet dualities.

Through materialization in objects and bodies, poetry is a carrier of social relations, a "thing" desired and trafficked in a market in conjunction with other things of value. Under authoritative discourses, whether articulated or presumed, poetry is subject to processes involving creation, preservation, repackaging, evaluation, derision, and so on. The market is my overarching framework for presenting a picture of poetry acting as a mediator in various facets of social life. This way to think about poetry takes us not just to literature but also to ethics, politics, history, religion, diplomacy, and overall paradigms for individual and communal existence.

I realize that the market metaphor as deployed here has the potential to become overdrawn. For this reason, I invoke it largely only when framing the discussions, in the interest of imparting a sophisticated understanding of a large and complex topic in very limited space. For readers who might find this grating on occasion, I can say that, at least in part, the analogy is meant to be tongue in cheek. By depicting poetic exchange as a market of goods and services, I hope also to denaturalize the way the market as an economic metaphor dominates our sense of the world today. Economic markets are never about finances alone, and this discussion of poetry may help to sensitize us to literary and other social products that undergird financial relationships. The market metaphor can take us to issues beyond what I discuss explicitly; I trust that readers will extend my suggestions to areas of interest to them.

The Element is divided into four sections. To provide a concrete sense for the place of poetry in the Persian world, I begin by presenting autobiographical elements from an author who was himself a poet and dedicated decades of his life to creating a lengthy work consisting of poets' life stories and samples of their work spanning a period of seven centuries (ca. 950–1650 CE). While stylized and conforming to genre, this narrative brings out poetry's enmeshment in subjectivity, interpersonal relations, and religious and sociopolitical patterns.

In the second section, I delve into Persian discussions that define poetry, elaborate on how and why it works, and comment on its valuation for social purposes. Rather than proceeding from a definition, I wish to emphasize that contestation on the very notion of poetry is a crucial part of the story. The theoretical discourse I highlight is culled from different social and professional locations and provides us the means to appreciate commonality and variation within the imagined community of interpretation.

The third section takes us to anthologies of poets' works and lives. In addition to introducing a few highly celebrated figures, narrative patterns for the poetic past indicate how poetic expression was turned into varied cultural memory with presumed inner momentum leading to apotheoses. The works I have chosen for this category sensitize us to issues concerning genealogy, hierarchy, and gender.

The last section of the Element takes up especially complex examples pertaining to poetry's social salience. I present works in composite genres (translation, history, memoir, and collections meant for self-fashioning) to highlight poetry's wide reach as discourse, practice, and authority in existential matters. Materials covered in this section are not usually treated in scholarship on Persian poetry. My choice to highlight them is part of the effort to show how, in the Persian world, poetry should be a part of the discussion in fields beyond literary history and theory.

Note on Usages

All non-English texts quoted in this Element are my own translations. In cases where English translations exist, I have retranslated based on my preferences. For poetry, I have chosen to use free verse for all genres rather than attempting to create a correspondence between Persian and English forms (e.g. heroic couplets or blank verse for *masnavi*, sonnet for *ghazal*, etc.). Assigning English genre terms to Persian poetic forms is generally a fraught matter and is beyond the scope of the current topic (Utas, 2008). While lack of meter and rhyme certainly distance the translations from the "feel" of the originals, I find that free verse is easiest on the ear and mind when encountering poetry in English today.

Names of peoples, places, and works are transliterated according to a highly simplified scheme. Consonants are represented as pronounced in Persian even when words may be of Arabic or other origin (e.g. "z" for *zay*, *dhay*, and *dhad*; "s" for *thay*, *sin*, and *sad*; etc.). Short vowels are given as "a," "e," "o," and long vowels as "ā," "i," and "u." Hamza and *'ayn* are represented by the apostrophe (') and single inverted comma (') respectively. The notation "b." as part of personal names means "son of" and "daughter of" (*ebn* or *bent*). Whenever available, I have used place names in their established English spellings, transliterating only when places are likely to be obscure to most readers. The first time a city or region is mentioned, I provide, in parentheses, the name of the modern country in which it is now located.

1 A Walk in Poetic Timespace

In the first half of the seventeenth century, Taqioddin Mohammad Awhadi-Balyāni (d. ca. 1640, hereafter Awhadi) produced a work on Persian poetry that is extraordinary on two counts. The first thing of note about the work, entitled *'Arafātol-'āsheqin va 'arasātol-'ārefin* (The Resurrection Ground of Lovers and the Courtyards of Knowers), is its length. Running to nearly 5,000 pages in one printed edition, it contains entries on more than 3,500 poets, distributed throughout Iran and Central and South Asia during seven centuries prior to the point of writing. Much of the text consists of citations of poetry. The work's sheer scope makes it perhaps the longest anthology cum biographical dictionary of Persian poets ever composed (Golchin-Ma'āni, 1984: 2:3–21).

The second noteworthy aspect of Awhadi's work is a distinctive organization that forefronts poetry as a unique form of verbal expression locatable in human lives. Departing from existing patterns for biographical dictionaries that I discuss later in this Element, Awhadi's scheme eviscerates calendrical time and mappable space. Instead, he asks the reader to accompany him on a stroll through a "poetry-scape" born of combining the order of the Arabic alphabet with poetry's development from the distant past to the author's present.

Awhadi imagines time as a vast ground akin to the plain of 'Arafat in Mecca that figures prominently in the annual rite of the hajj. During the pilgrimage, attendees are required to stand in this plain for several hours on one day as a preview for the resurrection promised for the end of time. In Islamic eschatology, God is expected to reconstitute all humans to be present at such a plain once the world has been dissolved. Awhadi's invitation to imagine time as a resurrection plain self-consciously mimics the divine function, except that his purview is limited to the segment of humanity that consists of Persian poets. As in the ultimate resurrection, Awhadi's resurrection collapses the normative sequencing of time and allows people from all periods to be present simultaneously in a single narrativized place.

The resurrection ground – a representation of embodied time consisting of poets' lives – is then split into twenty-eight courtyards that correspond to the letters of the Arabic alphabet (the additional four Persian letters are subsumed within the Arabic list). In this process, time that had first become space is now divided into the building blocks of language. Each courtyard/ letter is then further divided into three enclosures that contain poets divided between "the ancients" (*motaqaddemin*), the "middle ones" (*motavassetin*), and the "contemporaries" (*mota'akhkherin*). Poets are placed in the enclosures within the courtyards on the plain according to where their poetic names (*takhallos*) occur in alphabetical order (Awhadi, 2010: 1:32–36). The division into enclosures has a temporal structure, although the categorization is now subordinate to the rule of language. Time is first eliminated and then reestablished as a subcategory within the linguistic abstraction that is the alphabet.

Approached based on normative expectations regarding history, Awhadi's narrative is disorienting and possibly disconcerting. For example, on a single page, one can be asked to move to lives located centuries and vast distances apart. The unifying element, crucial to the narrative's success, is the author's judgment on poets and poetry. For the presentation to be efficacious, the reader must trust Awhadi as the articulator of poetic tradition. The anchor for this trust is the author's first-person voice, which is present in three separable forms in the narrative. First, the introduction contains a summary of his life story, highlighting his credentials as a poetic adjudicator. Second, he treats himself as an entry within his scheme and provides copious examples of his own poetry. He used the pen name "Taqi," so we find him in the "contemporary" enclosure in the courtyard of the letter *tay* (2:882–925). And third, his voice seeps through in numerous entries on others from his own time. He provides details for personal encounters and relationships, including stories of studentship, camaraderie, competition, and conflict.

Awhadi's picture of the world contemporary to him shows poets moving around extensively for reasons such as exile and alienation, seeking knowledge and training, and pursuing economic or social opportunities. The social prestige of Persian poetry is a stable field of endeavor in lives that, otherwise, appear quite insecure due to material circumstances as well as emotional states evoked constantly in the verses Awhadi cites. To convey a more particularized sense for the place of poetry in the Persian world, I will provide some details from Awhadi's self-representations. His circumstances as well as his encyclopedic familiarity with the literary corpus as it existed in the early seventeenth century can help us situate poetry in society. Moreover, this author's career exemplifies how poetic knowledge and prestige were acquired through a kind of practice-oriented education in courts and other prominent settings in society.

In the autobiographical narrative in the introduction, Awhadi states that he was born in Isfahan (Iran), on 3 Moharram, 973 AH (July 31, 1565 CE), into a family known for its religious accomplishments. He was an orphan at birth because his father had left for a journey to India after his conception and had then died, away from home, before the delivery. Awhadi claims that he weaned from his mother suddenly at the age of one and that – from that point to when he was writing at the age of fifty – he could remember almost everything that had passed in front of his senses "like etchings on stone" (1:18). This suggests an eidetic memory, which is plausible given the number and extent of citations provided in his work.

During his childhood, he benefited from a scheme instituted by Shah Tahmāsp (d. 1576), the reigning Safavid king in Iran. Based on a dream, this king had decreed that, in every city of his realm, he would bear the educational and living expenses of forty orphans who were Sayyeds (descendants of the Prophet Mohammad). Chosen for this charity, Awhadi excelled in school, avoiding frivolous games that were the norm for children. Successful over his peers in the religious and philosophical sciences, he had an aptitude for poetry as well. However, his mother and other guardians dissuaded him from it, considering it unserious and of lesser value as a career compared to the religious sciences that he was expected to master on account of his heritage and evident talent. In his entry on himself as a poet, he states that he became serious about poetry from the age of nine by starting to study commentaries by experts (2:883). Any qualms he may have retained on this ceased when his mother died when he was twelve and left him in the world without any immediate family (1:20).

The childhood part of Awhadi's narrative shows poetry to be a distinctive discourse in competition with other forms of remunerative literary activity. Especially in sixteenth-century Iran, Sayyeds could leverage their genealogy to acquire status among the powerful scholarly classes. For a person born with this privilege, going toward poetry was to trade an assured career for insecurity. Moreover, for some, poetry was morally suspect on intellectual as well as social grounds. To become involved in poetry was thus a risky prospect on multiple counts.

Between the ages of twelve and twenty, Awhadi spent time in the Iranian cities of Isfahan, Yazd, and Shiraz, becoming ever more adept at many kinds of learning. His inward concentration on the development of his connection to God led eventually to a vision of the Prophet Mohammad, a customary marker of divine favor. His description of the vision has few details, conveying an experience where he simply perceived a visual encounter with the Prophet's body. Especially for a Sayyed, a vision of the revered ancestor often acted as a form of initiation that ratified the genealogical distinction. Awhadi represents the vision as marking the moment when the status of his own body changed from being ordinary material to being that of someone who was truly alive. On the social side, when he reached maturity he was invited to become a part of the household of an uncle by marrying his daughter. While acknowledging the kindness toward an orphan, he declined the offer in order not to become tied down to an ordinary life (1:23–24).

At twenty, Awhadi joined the retinue of the Safavid king Mohammad Khodābandeh (d. 1595–6), Tahmāsp's successor, who was blind. He then traveled to various cities as a part of the court, acting as a poet as well as a repository able to recall verses by others. The political situation in Iran underwent a significant change when Shāh ʿAbbās (d. 1629) ascended the throne in 1588 and began major projects to consolidate and expand the empire.

Returning home after victories over bitter Central Asian rivals, 'Abbās decided to turn Isfahan into a great new capital city. In 1598, one night as the city's monuments were lit up with lamps, a competition was held for the best quatrain describing the scene. Awhadi claims that the competition was judged by the king himself and that he won it with the following verses:

> Isfahan's square, shining like the moon and the Pleiades,
>   casts a hundred marks on the chest of the highest celestial sphere.
> This is no illumination! Rather, spread in front of the king,
>   are stars fallen from the sky in poses of prostration.

(1:29)

After a few years with the court, Awhadi parted company from the Safavid establishment and spent some years traveling, with stays in Yazd, Isfahan, Qazvin, and Shiraz, in Iran, and Shi'i holy shrines in southern Iraq.

As shown in Awhadi's account of his youth and early adulthood, Persian poetry was a matter related to courts. We can substantiate this connection from the earliest times of sociopolitical investment in poetic production in the Persian world (Davis, 1999; Meisami, 1987: 3–39). In its widest form by the sixteenth century, this involved monarchs, princes and princesses, viziers, governors, and locally powerful people, all of them participating in an economy that was collaborative as well as competitive. A promising prospect such as Awhadi, as represented in his own description, was a sought-after person. But once a part of the system, he competed with others for attention and material resources. Courts in Iran were ambulatory, which led to travel and familiarity with literary scenes and celebrities based in various cities. Awhadi's time in the Safavid court amounted to the best form of poetic education one could garner in the field. He put this to extensive use when he composed his lengthy work decades later.

In Iran at the cusp between the sixteenth and seventeenth centuries, the highest rewards for poetic excellence were to be had in India. Under the Mughal dynasty, Persian was promoted heavily as a prestige language. Bigger and richer by orders of magnitude, and replete with competing courts, India was the cause of a perpetual poetic brain drain from Iran. Many poets left their natal land for good, while others circulated back and forth between the two regions (Sharma, 2017: 16–62).

True to pattern, in 1606, when he was in his early thirties, Awhadi too decided to go to India. He relates that he heard the news of the death of the Mughal king Akbar (d. 1605) during the journey. His first stop in India was Lahore (now Pakistan), where he stayed for a year and a half as a part of the court of Jahāngir (d. 1627), the new Mughal king. He then moved to Agra (India) together with the court. The same association led him to travel to Gujarat (India), where he spent three years. From Gujarat he wished to arrange a passage to Arabia via the sea to perform the hajj. This was unsuccessful, and he returned to Agra in 1611–12. He began composing his grand narrative of Persian poetry in Agra, working assiduously to complete the first draft during the period 1613–15 (1:30–32).

The arc of Awhadi's career indicates that he fell into the mainstream of poetically gifted individuals who could acquire at least a modicum of celebrity and its associated material benefits in both Iran and India. He saw himself as both a connoisseur of poetry and a practitioner who belonged to the highest echelons among his contemporaries. On the latter score, the ambition outpaced the outcomes, since he does not figure among the period's luminaries as reported by others. His entry devoted to himself is quite extensive, showcasing skill and imagination, although not the distinctiveness that would have allowed him to make a name in a crowded field (2:882–925). As in his reports on others, he quantifies his poetic output, saying that he had composed more than 40,000 verses, excluding about 12,000 whose written versions were lost at one point and which he could not reconstitute from memory. On top of all this, the *'Arafātol-'āsheqin* included 75,000 verses from others that he was able to cite (2:885). He was, then, a living repository of Persian verse whose written work materialized the treasure.

With respect to his poetic inclinations, Awhadi states that he had tried his hand at most forms of poetry. Unlike many others, he avoided writing praise poetry simply for financial gain or as satire, these being common parts of the competition among poets. The citations he provides of his own work include the following:

> Who am I – the heavenly king in the palace of speech!
> The enlightening sun, rising over speech's assembly.
> My verse is spiritual dew – no surprise that
> it waters speech's garden to green.
> In verses, the space separating hemstitches wouldn't be,
> save for my utterance's hand rending apart the collar of speech.
>
> *(2:915)*

The hyperbole of these verses is common fare in poetry from the period in which Awhadi was writing. Making speech into entities ("palace," "assembly," "garden," and a garment with a "collar" in quick succession) indexes Awhadi's general interest in treating poetic utterances as products under his curatorial and creative control (Schimmel, 1992).

Among Awhadi's reports on his contemporaries, stories of conflict and appreciation are most helpful to understand his world since they show interpersonal relations. For example, he describes extreme bitterness between poets named Jonuni Qandahāri and Aqdasi. Jonuni hailed from Kandahar

(Afghanistan) but had settled in Shiraz. He was a soldier, with special skill in archery, who would sometimes present himself very normally and at other times cultivate the appearance of being a pauper. His poetic name "Jonuni" means "one who has madness," indicating a degree of separation from society in the form of personal habits or cultivation of a persona. He had a dark complexion, which was sometimes a subject of ridicule in satire directed at him. He composed a lot, but the poetry was never made into a collection. He died in 1591 (2:1075–1077).

Aqdasi, Jonuni's nemesis, was originally from Mashhad (Iran) and had been led to spend a number of years in Shiraz. He was a man of very sharp wit, whom some mistook for a slave because his complexion and hair appeared Indian. After one fight with Jonuni, Aqdasi took to underhanded methods. He composed a highly offensive satire on prophets, saints, and other revered figures in Jonuni's voice. The verses contained the refrain "I am that Jonuni who . . . " so that the putative authorship would be prominent. Copying this out multiple times, he distributed it among people, hoping that it would lead to Jonuni's condemnation. But the ruse was discovered, and the verses became well-known as Aqdasi's composition. This led to a mob wanting to kill him. Awhadi states that he alerted Aqdasi to the danger, despite the fact that they were not on good terms, and helped him to escape from Shiraz to the Shi'i holy cities in Iraq. Awhadi met Aqdasi again later in Isfahan, by which time he had repudiated some of his earlier habits. He died of consumption in 1595–6 in Qazvin, at not more than twenty-six years of age (1:642–643).

The sense of poetry as a weapon is quite clear in this account. Poets' names were tied closely to their poetic outputs, and a skillful imitator could create havoc by corrupting the link. One key here is that Aqdasi had the skill to create a fake that he thought would besmirch his rival. This kind of subterfuge could not be implemented by an untalented person. But the market was smart enough not to fall for the fraud. Once discovered, the attempt at faking nearly led to the culprit's death on account of outrage from the victim as well as the general public. Physical and psychological portraits of poets Awhadi provides also indicate poetry's role in creating individualized identities. The pen names poets chose for themselves combined with external identifiers to create brands that acted as advertisements and sometimes needed defense in public (Losensky, 1998a).

Another instance of a bitter feud that some found entertaining involved the poets 'Arshi and Zamāni, both resident in Yazd. 'Arshi was a Kurdish nobleman, descended from Safavid kings on his mother's side and the famous Sufi master Ne'matollāh Vali on his father's. He lived a life of leisure, participating in the city's literary life. This positioning afforded independence since, for him, poetry was not the means to a livelihood.

The local scene in Yazd became especially energetic around 1591 (or 1595 –
Awhadi's reports on this in two different parts of the text do not match) when
plague broke out in Isfahan. A large number of poets, Awhadi among them,
left for Yazd to wait for it to subside, leading to a heightening of literary
activity there, including competition. Zamāni was a notorious figure in the
city, often getting into altercations with others. His dispute with 'Arshi was
especially pronounced, each claiming to be a better poet than his rival.
One day, someone put Awhadi on the spot by asking him his opinion on the
excellence of thought to be found in the work of the two. As he hesitated for
fear of becoming embroiled in an undesirable conflict, another person jumped
in to say that he would answer instead. He condemned both poets by opining
that the difference between the two was that Zamāni wished to compose good
poetry but could not, while 'Arshi could compose a lot of bad poetry and did
(3:1679–81; 5–2930–31).

In this instance, Awhadi's report points to the human geography of poetry.
The scene for poetic congregation changed from Isfahan to Yazd based on the
plague. In other cases, the same happened between other cities due to wars and
famine, political changes, and economic ups and downs. The production and
performance of poetry bore a close relationship to other forms of socioeconomic
production. Within social settings, poetic competition was connected to other
forms of rivalry and personal likes and dislikes. Those who were deemed
competent to judge the quality of poetry occupied a place that required sensi-
tivity to interpersonal and other politics quite aside from what they thought of
individuals on account of their literary talent.

Poetry was a matter connected closely to personal identity as well. One
evocative story regarding this involves the solitary struggle of a certain
Mawlāna 'Āref. He was originally from Shabankara (southern Iran) and had
first come to India during the reign of Akbar. He then returned to Iran and
subsequently came back to India during Jahāngir's rule, spending much time in
Bengal. Awhadi met him while accompanying the Mughal court, and the two
spent six months together traveling between Ajmer and Mandu. 'Āref had
compiled his poetry into a divan that amounted to 8,000–9,000 verses.
Awhadi remarks that 'Āref could be subject to melancholy and social
withdrawal.

He told the author that, many years before their meeting, he had once tried to
commit suicide. When Jahāngir was still a prince, he had once been angry at
'Āref and imprisoned him in a castle. Due to the afflictions brought by this
incarceration and the meanness of the guards, he developed madness and
extreme melancholy. One night he decided to kill himself by running a knife
across his own neck, as when animals are killed. For some reason, the cut spared

the artery. He took this to be an omen against his original intention and jumped into a pool of freezing water to stop the bleeding. When he came out, he was saved, and the guards were amazed. The experience cured him of madness, dissolved the black bile that was causing the melancholy, and put him on the path of repentance and rehabilitation (5:2837–2838).

Relationships between poets could be based on tremendous affection and respect as well. In this context, Awhadi speaks of his own great admiration for two celebrities of the time: Vahshi-Bāfqi (d. 1583) and 'Orfi-Shirāzi (d. 1591). When young, Awhadi imitated Vahshi-Bāfqi's style, regarding him as the ultimate exemplar of the kind of poetry that was then in fashion. He eventually acted as Vahshi-Bāfqi's literary executor, collecting his verses into a divan that included 9,000 verses in a whole host of poetic forms (7:4581). While Vahshi-Bāfqi lived and died in Yazd, 'Orfi-Shirāzi started in Shiraz and died in Lahore after an extensive career in India. Awhadi says that when he went to Shiraz in his youth, he spent time in 'Orfi-Shirāzi's company, five years before the great poet undertook his journey to India. This means that he met the poet in 1579. He tells us that everyone who was attempting to compose in the 'fresh' (*tāzeh*) style popular at the time took 'Orfi-Shirāzi to be the model (Beers, 2015; Kinra, 2015: 201–240; Losensky, 1998b: 134–192).

Awhadi's work provides for us a sense of poetry as a kind of flow of felicitous language between people. His scheme for the work's divisions highlights transferences across three groups arranged diachronically (ancients, middle ones, contemporaries). His own life story, and what we pick up regarding the lives of his contemporaries, shows transferences between teachers and students, originators and imitators, rivals in heated competition, and people in sympathy with each other. Even as it focuses intensively on poetry as a special domain, this lengthy work reminds us consistently of other aspects of life such as politics and economics. Seen through this vantage point, Awhadi's *'Arafātol-'āsheqin va 'arasātol-'ārefin* turns poetry into a lens to think about the Persian world as a sociocultural arena in the widest sense.

The most appropriate way to end this short tour through Awhadi's massive work is to provide some more of his own poetry. The following is a translation of verses that encapsulate a number of prominent topoi of Persian poetry permeating the tradition he attempted to memorialize in his grand work:

> In a festival of union
>   the stricken heart has no place.
> No hospital with cures
>   holds someone afflicted with love.
> An eye lit up,
>   fueled by the oil of hopeless tears,

has a fullness that leaves
no space for luminescence.
Your love encircles
my heart in such a way,
fidelity is all that
it can now hold.
If it weren't apostasy,
I would say this:
you and I melded into one –
even God cannot squeeze in.

(2:908)

2 Weights and Measures

Writing in the early thirteenth century, 400 years before Awhadi began pouring his prodigious memory onto paper, the literary critic Shams-e Qays Rāzi (d. ca. 1230) tells his readers that evaluators of poetry should be careful about sharing their opinions. This is because, in the day, there was no profession more debased and despised than theirs. While everyone agreed that crafts other than poetry required long, assiduous effort, people who had studied a few poems felt justified to set themselves up as poets and start spewing drivel. People like that had such a high opinion of their own output that when someone suggested otherwise, they took it to be jealousy and became abusive.

Shams-e Qays Rāzi illustrates the situation with an experience of his own. A few years earlier when he was in Bukhara (Uzbekistan), a local religious scholar had attached himself to him. Even after five to six years of instructional effort, he could not do any better than compose bad poetry that was the butt of jokes. Many years later, Shams-e Qays Rāzi came across this man in Marv (Turkmenistan), where he proceeded to recite a bad composition. Acting in the manner of a doctor, Shams-e Qays Rāzi asked him to explain the meaning. The explanation was even more nonsensical and led people to snigger. He then went away and came back with verses that were yet worse.

The same thing happened again another day when Shams-e Qays Rāzi was fasting and they happened to meet in private. Moved by compassion due to being in a religious state, he said to him: "You are a sincere man and have proven your rights on me from your devotion. I do not like that you say verses without understanding. What you say is not good. This leads me and others to laugh, which disgraces us. Listen to my advice and stop writing poetry." The man said that he understood and that he would cease.

While Shams-e Qays Rāzi thought that he had done a good deed, the man had actually taken offense and wrote an invective against him. Many years later,

Shams-e Qays Rāzi discovered the verses the man had composed and spread around among his enemies:

> From jealousy, Shams-e Qays said to me:
> "Your poetry is bad, don't compose more."
> I wanted to say to him: "O asinine one,
>   you are hardly the one to point to people's errors.
> Given that you claim to be a poet and a prosodist,
>   try saying even a couplet better than mine.
> Failing that, stop faulting the poetry of another,
>   who will satirize you, rendering you a menstruation rag."

Amounting to doggerel, these verses denounced Shams-e Qays Rāzi as a judge of poetry and prosody and crudely compared him to a rag used by a woman to soak up menstrual blood. The verses satisfy technical standards for being poetry but possess no coherence or wit even with respect to being mean to someone. Shams-e Qays Rāzi says, "The benefit of the advice I had given him, out of compassion, was that satire and abuse against me were to be found in notebooks throughout [Persian] Iraq and Khorasan" (Shams-e Qays Rāzi, 2010: 455).

This account is instructive for showing that Persian poetry was a prominent arena of cultural and literary endeavor by the early thirteenth century. Production in Persian came in the wake of a long history of similar positions held by literary Arabic and other languages that had developed into prominent loci for cultural expression and competition in earlier centuries. As an entity of value, poetry was a part of the market of ideas and goods, which meant also that it had to have standards. Inasmuch as poetry was made up of common words utilized across a vast region, its regulation could only be through a discursive consensus among producers and consumers that was maintained through people or texts accepted as authorities. This is the role Shams-e Qays Rāzi occupies in the story, somewhat akin to that of an umpire in a game who is trusted as a judge based on knowledge of rules. But he had no power to punish or restrict any practitioner of poetry, save through giving advice. Experts like him were necessary for there to be a shared literary arena, but they could easily become objects of anger and abuse, if their judgments were not to the liking of one or another party. Shams-e Qays Rāzi registers resignation about this being the double reality of poetic adjudication in his context.

In the remainder of this section, I present a number of discussions on the nature of Persian poetry that were composed during the twelfth and thirteenth centuries. My hope is to provide a sense of the variety of issues that pertained when Persian poetic expression was evaluated in the Middle Ages. The corpus of Persian poetry as it existed by this time was extensive enough to be made the subject of deep analysis. This included discussion on literary technicalities as well as social, psychological, and religious functions imbricated in poetry. My greatest interest here is not in definitions of poetry as such, which existed but matter little for thinking about society. Rather, I focus on representations in theory and usage that provide a picture for poetry as a social matter. The examples I have chosen help us to understand poetry's place in transactions involving ideas and material goods that constituted the market I am attempting to describe.

The narratives I discuss here belong to varied genres: a manual meant for learned secretaries; a compendium on rules, techniques, and styles for composing poetry; the earliest work to anthologize preeminent poets by describing their lives and providing samples of their work; and hagiography of a Sufi figure who is described as having "lived" by poetry. The diversity of genres is important to register in order to appreciate poetry as a contested affair. The value assigned to a particular poetic work could differ greatly based on evaluators' intellectual and social commitments as well as the context in which the work had been produced.

2.1 Poetry as Political Instrument

Ahmad b. 'Omar Nezāmi 'Aruzi of Samarkand (Uzbekistan) composed his *Chahār Maqāleh* (Four Discourses) around the middle of the twelfth century. The work is meant to guide people seeking to join courts in Central Asia and Iran as scribes, secretaries, bureaucrats, and royal boon companions. The work's four sections describe what is required of four types of courtiers: literary secretaries, poets, astrologers, and physicians. The author speaks on the basis of his knowledge of the past as well as his personal experience, which he interpolates to make his points. His chosen pen name, 'Aruzi, means 'prosodist', giving us a sense of his high investment in poetic matters. His ultimate aim is to present a picture of poetry's role in statecraft, which is meant to help aspiring poets as they cultivate prospects.

'Aruzi's discussion on poets in the *Chahār Maqāleh* begins by defining poetry as a type of linguistic practice tied to human psychology:

> Poetry is the art used by the poet to correlate, via analogy, between initial imagination and deductions. [This is a] pathway for aggrandizing small things and diminishing what is great, which re-upholsters good into evil and makes evil appear good. Manipulation of imagination causes the rise of powers of anger and lust, leading temperaments to delight or become depressed. Thus, great occurrences are made to come about in the world.
>
> ('Aruzi, 1910: 42)

This highly abstract description – in which it is difficult to tell whether the author is recommending or condemning poetry – is concretized through a series of anecdotes that make clear that he sees poetry as a necessary ingredient in politics in multiple ways. He first tells the story of an ordinary herdsman who one day heard some verses that inflamed his passions. He sold all his animals and went off on a military spree until the point of becoming the head of an army and ruling over a number of cities. From this we gather that poetry is a necessary element for people to imagine themselves outside of their familiar circumstances. Hyperbole intrinsic to poetic expression can lead to endeavors that might seem impossible or inadvisable under "prosaic" conditions. Poetry is therefore a crucial ingredient in creating political change and development.

Just as it can ignite someone to become a political leader, poetry is essential on the other end of the cycle, when great political acts need memorialization. 'Aruzi provides a long list of poets whose productions correlate with the careers of rulers and dynasties. He reinforces the point through verses that mention Mahmud of Ghazni (d. 971), a ruler whose conquests as well as patronage for poets were legendary:

> What a number of palaces Mahmud built,
>> contending with the moon in their grandeur.
> Not a brick from them you will now see.
>> What remains, instead, is 'Onsori's panegyric.
>
> *(46)*

The king mentioned in these verses is the subject of other anecdotes as well. These include one highly celebrated story describing the experiences of Abol-Qāsem Ferdowsi (d. 1020), author of the epic *Shāhnāmeh* (Book of Kings). 'Aruzi claims that this poem – the most celebrated work of Persian poetry of all time – came about after twenty-five years of effort on the poet's part. But when it was presented to Mahmud, court intrigues arranged themselves such that the king failed to disburse the grand reward Ferdowsi expected to receive as a show of appreciation for the way he had memorialized Persian kingship. This led Ferdowsi to transfer his allegiance to another, lesser ruler and to write a satire on Mahmud. Much later, Mahmud was led to rue his treatment of Ferdowsi, following which he sent the treasure to the poet. As camels carrying the goods entered the city from one gate, Ferdowsi's funeral procession was leaving from another gate (74–81).

The dissatisfaction Ferdowsi suffered represented a breakdown in the presumed social contract that existed between poets and great rulers. The tragic nature of the reception of his poetry fed into Ferdowsi's legend, amalgamating with his conceptualization of the poet as a kind of epic hero whose exploits paralleled the fates of the royal figures described in his work (Davidson, 2013). In the long term, Ferdowsi's *Shāhnāmeh* became a celebrated classic, including being the subject of a large fund of fine manuscript paintings (see Figure 2).

'Aruzi's work shows a deep interdependence between the functions of rulers and poets. Much of the section on poets in the *Chahār Maqāleh* describes what the poet needs to succeed under the base understandings of poetry's potency he provides. Contending that "poetry is useful in all sciences and all sciences are useful in poetry," he recommends cultivating wide knowledge (47). Breadth of competence helps poets to create verses that are rhetorically compelling, through which they are then able to induce rulers to undertake the needful. The ability to modulate moods through poetic expression is an important power, since rulers need to be brought out of melancholy, excessive passion, temperamental inaction, sedentariness, and other states. Providing details of one of his own successes, he ranks spontaneity among the highest abilities in the poet's craft. A poet able to create verses immediately, appropriate to the occasion at hand, has the highest chance of being noticed and appreciated by a political authority (81–84).

Corresponding with the needs of his intended audience, 'Aruzi's approach to poetry is fundamentally functional and instrumentalist. Based on a psychological theory, he takes poetry's political efficacy to be an established fact. With this in mind, he proceeds to show, primarily through examples, how aspiring poets may make names for themselves as well as earn fortunes. The mutual dependence between rulers and poets can be mapped to a social field in which both sides could be assertive despite the apparent clear hierarchy between patrons and craftspeople (Sharlet, 2011).

2.2 Rules for Composition

Shams-e Qays Rāzi, whom we met at the beginning of this section, lived about half a century after 'Aruzi. His *Mo'jam fi ma'āyir-e ash'ār-e 'Ajam* (Compendium of Measures for Persian Poetry) counts among the earliest systematic descriptions of technical and rhetorical standards for Persian poetic composition. This work contains lengthy discussions on topics such as meters, rhythms, rhymes, repetition, rhetorical figures, and felicitous and infelicitous usages, all explained through copious examples (Landau, 2013).

Shams-e Qays Rāzi's approach to poetry is that of a critic invested in methodical evaluation. His overarching view is that "poetry consists of instruments, and writing poetry proceeds from initial propositions. In the absence of these, no poetry can be called good, and no poet can be designated by that title. Poetry is called good when the instruments of poetry – correct phrases, pleasant

Figure 2 "Goshtāsp Slays the Dragon of Mount Saqila," folio from the
Shāhnāmeh (Book of Kings) of Shāh Tahmāsp, attributed to Mirzā 'Ali,
Iran, Tabriz, ca. 1530–5, opaque watercolour, ink, and gold on paper, 45 × 30 cm.
© The Aga Khan Museum, AKM 163.

words, and eloquent expressions and subtle meanings – are embodied into
meters, leading to the production of a stream of verses" (443). This understanding starts from a place quite different from 'Aruzi's instrumentalist approach,
even though the two authors use many of the same exemplars to make their
points.

For Shams-e Qays Rāzi, poetry comes about on the basis of established rules and patterns that are presumed to preexist instantiation. The rules cover the gamut between forms (meters, rhymes, etc.), aesthetic judgments, and semantic value. Shams-e Qays Rāzi writes further that "meaning without expression has no vitality, and expression without meaning pleases no one. ... Words are vessels for meanings, and meanings are their valuables. Speech that has no subtle meaning, to which those with discerning temperaments might incline, is like an empty vessel devoid of objects of value" (456).

Shams-e Qays Rāzi's views on form and content indicate that someone who does not know rhyme and meter has no means of producing speech that would be called poetry. But, equally significantly, one could not be a poet by dint of knowing the technicalities alone. As in the case of the man who ended up maligning Shams-e Qays Rāzi by calling him a rag for menstrual blood, verses that are neither aesthetically pleasing nor generatively meaningful are not poetry. While basic rules pertaining to forms can be learned through memorization, aesthetic and semantic values are inculcated through apprenticeship and long exposure. These bear fruit only if a person has innate aptitude for poetry. This point is helpful for distinguishing between versification – which almost anyone could do by following the rules – and genuine poetic composition.

Shams-e Qays Rāzi further notes that being a talented poet and evaluating poetry are separate vocations: "There is plenty a poet who writes good poetry but cannot critique properly, and many a critic of poetry who is incapable of writing good poetry. They asked a leading theologian why he did not compose poetry. He said, 'What I want does not come to me, and what does come, I do not want'" (458). The difference is rooted in the fact that poets arrange speech by combining their instinctive inclinations with what is appropriate for circumstances at hand. In comparison, critics evaluate by coldly looking at how the words combine to create meanings, irrespective of who was the writer and how much effort went into the work.

Noting that "a verse is the poet's child," Shams-e Qays Rāzi opines that, even when poets know that someone else's composition is objectively superior to their own, they cannot bring themselves to understand that as being better. In comparison, "the critic suffers no heartburn on account of poetry by others who have tortured their minds organizing and coordinating between words and their meanings. S/he adopts whatever is found good and passes over whatever is flimsy" (459).

One of Shams-e Qays Rāzi's further points is that the crucial interdependency between words and meanings has particular repercussions for how poets might utilize existing poetry that was produced by others. Since verses are like poets' children, they have rights of ownership over them. But here poetry's specific nature is the source of a difference in how ownership might transfer. Shams-e Qays Rāzi writes that if a poet takes a verse that has a good match between words and meanings and imitates to the effect of creating something that is worse, then this has to be regarded as the imitating poet having stolen something from the originator. However, if the imitating poet understands the meanings of the verses correctly and then provides words to convey that meaning in a way better than the original, then the ownership of the meaning transfers to the imitator. The first producer nevertheless retains the right to be remembered as the originator (468–469).

This principle indicates that, from the perspective of a poetic critic, words that can be read are more significant than the meanings they convey on their own. The point is well taken in that most meanings expressed in poetry can be explained in prose as well. Since that does not render prose into poetry, better poetic words are markers of greater value in poetic assessments. And if poetry does express meanings that cannot be had any other way, then the source of that must be the words that constitute the expression. This leads Shams-e Qays Rāzi to a specific view on poetic plagiarism, versus the same occurring in other kinds of literary expression.

An analogy from Shams-e Qays Rāzi that is especially useful for thinking about poetry as a market commodity pertains to the manufacture of clothing. He states that poets are like weavers who create beautiful garments, with patterns and decorations, out of language. Their job ends once the garment has been made. The process of assigning value to the garments belongs to "brokers and cloth merchants who have handled countless garments of all types and merchandise from all countries. Only they know what is worthy of the treasuries of kings and how every type fits with the valuations of every class of people" (458). If weavers were to be the ones to put prices on things, they would completely lose track of their craft and spend all their time trying to figure out the economic particulars of elements such as labor and materials that went into weaving. Weavers can only put a price on their own work in isolation. Evaluation, however, is a comparative exercise that requires thorough acquaintance with a variety of possibilities.

The three elements I have collated from Shams-e Qays Rāzi's extensive work aggregate into an approach to poetry that consistently prioritizes the external surface of the text available to someone placed in the position of an evaluating critic. He acknowledges the special labors that poets themselves undertake. He is also mindful that "pretty words" alone do not make for good poetry. But for him poetry *qua* poetry is a matter of words ordered in ways that are precise as to rules, pleasing in terms of their effect, and maximally efficacious with respect to the desired meaning. This approach to poetry is reflected in numerous later works, including Mohammad b. Badr Jājarmi's *Mu'nesol-ahrār fi daqā'eqol-ash'ār* (The Free Men's Companion to Subtleties of Poems), an anthology organized by forms of poetry with samples. This work is extant in a remarkable autograph manuscript, with paintings, dated to 1341 (see Figure 3).

2.3 Poetic Knowledge

Working almost exactly contemporaneously with Shams-e Qays Rāzi, Mohammad 'Awfi is credited with the earliest surviving compilation of poetry, presented together with comments on poets' lives. Between Shams-e Qays Rāzi's compendium on technicalities and 'Awfi's work on the lives of poets, we can regard the early thirteenth century as a period of consolidation for Persian poetry as a literary tradition. 'Awfi was born in Bukhara into an influential family and spent his early professional years in the Qarakhanid court in Samarkand. Anticipating the arrival of the Mongols in Central Asia, he moved to India circa 1210. He wrote the *Lobābol-albāb* (Kernel of Kernels) while employed at the court of Nāseroddin Qabācheh (ruled 1210–28) in Multan (now Pakistan).

Before proceeding to the lives and poetic samples that make up the lengthy *Lobābol-albāb*, 'Awfi provides a general description of poetry and its significance. As pointed out in other recent scholarship, 'Awfi's musings on poetry have philosophical undercurrents that deserve greater attention than they have received (Keshavmurthy, 2011). His views on poetry as a carrier of knowledge add substantively to our understanding of poetry's valuation in the Persian world throughout the Middle Ages.

'Awfi's direct definition of poetry pertains to epistemology:

> From the perspective of language, you must know that poetry means knowledge, meaning wisdom. That is, the wisdom that can be apprehended by those who are sagacious, their perception being able to encompass it. The poet is the knower, meaning wise person, who apprehends astute meanings and is able to convey them in a way available to others who are knowledgeable. And an astute meaning denotes that which thought brings into being, from behind the mind's curtain, into subtle imagination.
>
> ('Awfi, 1906: 15)

Poetry in this explanation is an end product that comes to exist through a type of mental sublimation shared between wise people who can produce or apprehend it. It is created by thought as actor. Thought first extracts subtle imagination from the mind and then clothes such imagination with words representing

Figure 3 "Moon Entering the House of the Twelve Zodiac Signs." Folio from a copy of Jājarmi's *Mu'nesol-ahrār fi daqā'eqol-ash'ār*. Isfahan, Iran, 1341. Ink, opaque watercolor, and gold on paper: 16.8 × 23.2 cm. Cora Timken Burnett Collection of Persian Miniatures and Other Persian Art Objects, Bequest of Cora Timken Burnett, 1956. The Metropolitan Museum of Art, New York. 57.51.25.

shareable wisdom. For 'Awfi, poetry is the noblest form of a particular kind of knowledge, one that, like water of eternal life, persists over generations even as human beings live and die.

One way to understand 'Awfi's emphasis is to see it as the inverse of Shams-e Qays Rāzi's view discussed already. While Shams-e Qays Rāzi also understood poetry as language that connected appropriate words to worthwhile meaning, for him the outward linguistic element was paramount because this is what becomes the main object for a literary critic. For 'Awfi, the inward meaning, encapsulated in poetic words, constitutes an essential wisdom that runs through creation. Poets, then, are those who hook into this stream of knowledge and bring it out in a form (that is, poetry) that is shareable with those others who have the capacity to apprehend such knowledge.

'Awfi's definition for poetry stems from a cosmology that relates to the way God chose to create the world. The division of the earth's surface into land and water is parallel to the division of speech into prose and poetry. This parallelism plays on the word *bahr*, a homonym for bodies of water and poetic meter. This is not metaphorical usage in the strict sense because the two ideas represented by *bahr* do not hold places that are parallel within the encompassing contexts. Rather, the common word forms a suggestive link so that one might say that poetry as a generic concept is like a body of water. Some people – namely the poets – dive into poetry, made of meters, to retrieve verses that are object of value. This is parallel to the case of divers going underwater to bring out pearls and other treasures.

Lilting language, formed of words put into meters, is akin to water that moves in waves. Subtle meanings, which are the ultimate contents of poetry, are brought out by poets' diving minds. Vocalization of poetry then presents the subtle meanings to others who, although they did not undertake the dangerous work of diving, have the capacity to absorb the wisdom. The hidden origin of truths brought out by poets parallels the hidden presence of pearls in the sea. Much like pearls, poetic utterances retain a degree of mystery and obscurity even after they have become apparent (6–7).

'Awfi's proof for his understanding of poetry is a Hadith report (a saying attributed to Mohammad). The Prophet is supposed to have said: "God has treasures under his Throne, whose keys are the tongues of poets." This statement stands in contrast with Mohammad's vehement insistence that he himself was not a poet. Indeed, the fact that he was a true prophet excluded him from the category of being a poet in the absolute sense. This is because prophets have to be explicit and completely truthful under all circumstances, conveying the messages imparted to them through revelation without inserting their own linguistic inventiveness. Comparatively, poets seek hidden knowledge by diving into the sea of language. Their poetic products retain a level of allusiveness under all circumstances. In 'Awfi's presentation, prophets like Mohammad are, quite simply, not allowed to talk in allusions and riddles, which precludes them from being poets. However, prophets can appreciate and recommend poets as carriers of a kind of truth whose possibility is built into the way God created the world.

In light of 'Awfi's understanding, poetry may be seen as a lie that conveys a higher truth. The sea analogy sets up poetry as a product of a transference that occurs when a human being, initially located on a vessel on water's surface, jumps in to retrieve an unseen treasure. Inasmuch as this transference is dictated by the way the world is constituted, poets are expected to undertake the work into perpetuity, since the treasure is inexhaustible. Moreover, the fact that poetry is made of tropes – similes, metaphors, allusions, allegories, and so on – means that its verbal form constantly replicates the "hidden to apparent" dynamic from which it originates. In other words, poets bring out pearls out of the sea to present to nonpoets. The recipients are then required to undertake their own "diving" into the language to get to meanings enveloped by the words. 'Awfi's view of the intimate relationship between poetry and knowledge is especially helpful to understand poetry's special place in Sufi expression in Persian.

2.4 Living by Poetry

Abu Sa'id Abil-Khayr (d. 1049) is much celebrated on account of being the first great Sufi master whose life became preserved in Persian hagiographical texts. Based in Mayhaneh (Turkmenistan), he was a well-known religious figure in his own time. His fame continued to spread after his death, especially when two hagiographical works, written by his descendants over the course of the next century, became classics of a genre that exploded in popularity and significance in later centuries (O'Malley, 2019).

The earliest accounts of Abu Sa'id's life make a point of saying that he composed very little poetry (Lotfollāh, 2006: 122). However, a significant corpus, which is thought to have accreted in later times, has become attached to Abu Sa'id's name. As suggested by Mohammad-Rezā Shafi'i Kadkani, the scholar who has edited both of the early hagiographies focused on Abu Sa'id, the poetry is likely to have accrued to Abu Sa'id because he is shown to have been extremely sensitive to Persian poetic utterances at crucial moments during his career (Ebn-e Monavvar, 2003: cvii). We may call this a case of someone who was affected by poetry in an exemplary way, setting up a pattern taken up by large numbers of people in later centuries (de Bruijn, 1997).

In hagiography, exposure to poetry is described as being crucial to igniting Abu Sa'id's interest in Sufi practice. His father was part of a group that would occasionally gather to listen to music for religious purposes. When Abu Sa'id was very young, his mother suggested to his father that he should take the child with him so that the boy might develop an interest. During the performance, an extraordinary condition overcame the dervishes, and they began to dance ecstatically when the singer performed the following verses:

> This love, indeed, is a gift given to dervishes.
> Killing themselves is their show of allegiance.
> Men's status is not dinars and dirhams.
> The work of the chivalrous is to self-sacrifice.
>   *(Ebn-e Monavvar, 2003: 16)*

When the event was over, Abu Sa'id asked his father why the dervishes had been so affected by these verses. The father told him to be silent, with the admonition that the boy could not understand this and had no business asking the question. In later life, Abu Sa'id would recite these verses often and remarked that, if his father were still alive, Abu Sa'id would tell his father that, even as an adult at that time, he had not understood what had been sung that day.

It is worthwhile to think through how the relationship between poetic utterances and their meanings works in this story. At the base level, the words Abu Sa'id heard are quite straightforward. But put together, they make up verses whose message regarding love and self-sacrifice is enigmatic as well as drastic in terms of what is being asked of the dervishes. Further, why do the verses cause the dervishes to go into ecstasy and dancing? The corporeal response has no obvious relationship to the words' literal meanings, leading to the conclusion that they are conditioned to interpret the verses in a certain way at the communal level. We might well imagine a precocious child intrigued by all this, leading to the question to the father. The response – to be silent – adds another level of enigma rather than solving the problem of meaning.

The story's overall effect is that a chasm separates the verses' literal signification and their psychosomatic and social effects. The Sufi community, constituted through the ritual of audition, is the key mediatory element bridging the chasm. Abu Sa'id's comment that his father was dismissive because he did not know what to say stands in contrast with his own status as a great Sufi master who could explain the issues to his disciples. The poetic utterance, performed in song and amenable to vast differences in meaning, sits at the center of the two communities (one that Abu Sa'id experienced as a child, the other over which he presided as an adult) present in the story.

Hagiographical representation states that, as Abu Sa'id grew older, he became attached to a Sufi guide. This guide asked the young man if he wished to talk to God. When Abu Saʻid said yes, the guide instructed him that whenever he was in seclusion, he should repeatedly recite nothing but the following verses:

> Without you, beloved, I cannot be content.
> Beyond counting are the favors you have bestowed.
> Were every hair on my body to become a tongue,
>   the thanks I would give would still be a thousandth
>   of what should be done.
> *(Ebn-e Monavvar, 2003: 19; Lotfollāh, 2006: 117)*

In this instance, too, the words that comprise the verses are easily understandable. They are being recommended as discourse to be repeated constantly, made poignant by the fact that the message they contain is pointing to language's absolute inadequacy when it comes to the task of communicating with God. Here poetry is language that is necessary while also lacking effectiveness as to its content.

The only hagiographical story in which Abu Saʻid is shown to actually compose poetry (rather than to react to it or recite verses by others) involves a disciple who had fallen ill and was bedridden. Coming to know of this, Abu Saʻid asked one of his attendants to grab paper and pen and to take down something that could be sent to the ill man. He then composed a quatrain:

> O houri, rise and behold my artwork.
> Astonished, the guardian angel of paradise claps hands.
> A black mole throws a garment on those cheeks.
> In fear, the abdāl stretches his hand to the book.
> *(Ebn-e Monavvar, 2003: 275)*

Hearing these verses, the ill man recovered immediately and stood up from the bed.

Once again, the literal meaning of the verses in this story has no obvious relationship to the effects they induce within the story. They paint an allusive scene in which something powerful is being revealed, whose beauty is meant to be an object of wonder by a houri (a nymph-like being who resides in paradise) and a guardian angel. The beauty also seems to be the source of dread, instigating a spiritually high-ranked person (abdāl) to seek protection by reaching out to touch the Quran.

In the story, the quatrain works like a healing incantation, its power hidden underneath a nonobvious text but tied to Abu Saʻid's ability to understand the disciple's affliction and to cure it by sending a missive in coded language. These verses' prophylactic function had a long life as, over the centuries, the quatrain became associated generally with healing rituals among Sufis. And the verses' allusive message came to have a life all its own as they became the subject of at least twelve commentaries by major Sufi authors writing through the Middle Ages (Ebn-e Monavvar, 2003: cxix–cxxvii).

I will provide one further instance of the effects of poetry on Abu Saʻid. This one leads us to the market. One day, as he was in the bazaar, the master heard a slave girl singing the following verses:

> Today, there is no friend for me in this city.
> Brought to the market, and no buyer for me.
> The one who buys does not suit me.
> The one I wish, cannot buy me.
> *(Lotfollāh, 2006: 153–154)*

These verses so affected Abu Saʻid that he took out his carpet and sat down on site. He then asked that the slave girl be brought to him. When she came, he asked her to say the verses again. She did that, and Abu Saʻid did not ask her anything further. Instead, he inquired if her owner was available. When he came, he asked the price at which he would sell her. He said 1,000 dinars, to which Abu Saʻid agreed. Once the deal was done, he asked the girl who was her beloved. She indicated who the man was, upon which Abu Saʻid had him fetched and then married him to the girl.

In this case, the verses are different from the previous stories since they do evocate the problem that gets solved. Their precise meaning in context is, however, still related to a desire hidden in the girl's heart. While others may think that the girl is singing a commonplace song, Abu Saʻid is able to divine her thoughts simply by hearing her sing and then say the verses again a second time. He then grants her the wish, encapsulated in her plaintive song, by buying her freedom. Abu Saʻid understands the verses as performed and then rescues her using hard cash. His hagiographical persona is replete with stories of great generosity toward all. This story is, therefore, paradigmatic of his ability to expend material resources to ease life's burdens for others.

2.5 Poetic Words and Meanings

The materials I have presented in this section tell us that poetry's special qualities as an expressive linguistic form were apt to be understood in a variety of ways in the Persian world. The differences at work here can be summarized by comparing how the authors understand the relationship between poetic utterances and their meanings.

'Aruzi, the first author, is invested in poetry's sociopolitical efficacy. For him, poetry accomplishes a certain type of work with respect to human psychology, its effects being especially significant for those in positions of political power.

Poetry is an instrument whose inner workings we are able to deduce through the functions we know it to serve in public life. His effort is to help poets understand what kind of verses are best suited for creating desired sociopolitical effects.

For a literary critic like Shams-e Qays Rāzi, the psychological-political understanding might have seemed to miss the point about what is specific to poetry. He places the greatest emphasis on the words that make up poetry. While he reinforces the significance of meanings that must reside in worthwhile poetic utterances, this is for him a second-order concern. Language could be tremendously meaningful but would not qualify as poetry if it did not follow the rules of rhyme, meter, accepted usages, and so on. In poetry, then, an evaluation of words had to precede any considerations of meaning. This is an admonition well worth keeping in the forefront of modern assessments of Persian poetry as well (Beelaert, 2019).

For 'Awfi, the third author, poetry is a linguistic practice that hooks into a cosmological store of knowledge present in the world due to God's creative choice. The fact that poetry is the only way to access this form of wisdom gives the outward technical aspect of poetry an extraordinary status. This means that proper form is essential. The reason for this is not a set of historically evolved rules (as true for Shams-e Qays Rāzi) but meanings that materialize cosmic wisdom according to a divine plan forever embedded in the cosmos.

The case of Abu Sa'id's hagiographies is closest to the perspective we see in 'Awfi, except that here the emphasis shifts to social and salvational effects of hidden wisdom. Knowledge sought and put into operation through poetry is predicated on the existence of extraordinary individuals who are central to Sufi practice. Such individuals are affected by poetry to understand meanings far beyond the obvious. They can also turn poetry into a spell that provides cures and protection. A great saintly figure like Abu Sa'id then acts as a broker transacting across words and meanings. The traffic between words and correct meanings requires the presence of people like him.

3 Producers, Aggregators, Buyers

We have already been introduced to two works that correlate between poets' lives and their verses. I began the Element by describing the complex organization of data pertaining to poets found in Awhadi's *'Arafātol-'āsheqin va 'arasātol-'ārefin* and, in the section on valuation, discussed introductory comments on poetry found in 'Awfi's *Lobābol-albāb*. This genre of works figures prominently in the discussion since it consists of aggregative accounts that are repositories of social memory relevant for discussing poetry as a kind of market that persisted for centuries. The present section is focused entirely on representations of poets' biographies as windows on the production and consumption of poetry.

In approaching biographical dictionaries, I understand historical projections as products of a present in which authors create pasts for particular ends. I do not see time as a homogeneous and unstoppable flow. Rather, it is a narrative product manufactured as the past. As I discuss elsewhere in detail, evidence that allows us to think about time in this way abounds in materials pertaining to Persian, and more broadly Islamic, pasts (Bashir, forthcoming 2022). This applies overwhelmingly in the case of biographical collections dedicated to Persian poets. Awhadi's eclectic scheme for spacetime is a good case in point. To broaden the field, I provide details from three other works that are quite different from each other on account of their framing. Together, they illustrate the play between personal lives of poetic virtuosi, social patterns inscribed into literary genres, and political and economic factors pertaining to poetic production.

My treatment of the three works I have chosen toggles between attending to their structures – where the authors create their versions of narrative progression – and reviewing notices on prominent poets that help densify our awareness of poetry as an aspect of the Persian world. In the texts, we encounter the framings first since they are explained in the works' introductions. Notices on individual poets are then pegged to the frame as we read into the work. However, it is important to note that, when we think about how these works were put together, the knowledge of poetry and poets' lives preceded the creation of a narrative frame. That is, authors of biographical dictionaries first knew of the field through its exemplars, whether of old or active in their own milieu. The narrative structures they created were abstractions evolved out of particularized knowledge. The consistency (or lack thereof) between framings and individual biographies is an issue worth noticing in itself.

I would like to emphasize at the outset that calling the works I have chosen "biographical dictionaries" is an approximation. If we approach these works like one might modern encyclopedias or biographical projects (for example, the *Oxford Dictionary of National Biography*) we will assuredly be disappointed. The lives and works we are presented with here are not meant to give us the basics of a person's work or their overall trajectories in life. As evident from statements found commonly in the texts, the reader is supposed to be already familiar with the people under description. The notices rely on presumed prior knowledge to highlight issues that eventually lead to particular images of people that are in line with authors' stated aims for composing their compilations. These images are also oriented toward the future, meant to act as a memory aid for later generations. The works are, then, parts of larger conversations connected to social settings not accessible to us. The compilations are also interrelated, building on or correcting each other, creating a diachronic, deeply intertextual tradition.

In reading biographical dictionaries, it is helpful to think of our position as that of someone eavesdropping on a telephone conversation, where our access is limited to a single voice. However, we have to know that the person talking has an audience on the other end of the line, with whom he or she shares knowledge of other people. Our interpretation can, therefore, never be exhaustive. What we are able to say about the contents of the works is provisional by definition.

In what follows, I take up the three works one by one, focusing on entries that are especially interesting for my purposes. The works are: Dowlatshāh Samarqandi's *Tazkeratosh-sho'arā* (Memorial of Poets), composed in 1487 in Herat (Afghanistan); Sām Mirzā Safavi's *Tohfeh-ye Sāmi* (Sām's Gift), completed in Iran around 1560; and Soltān Mohammad Fakhri-Heravi's *Javāherol-'ajā'eb* (Wondrous Gems), composed in Sind (now Pakistan) circa 1555.

3.1 Generations

Dowlatshāh Samarqandi's introduction to the *Tazkeratosh-sho'arā* laments that, up until his time, Persian poets as a class had not received coverage adequate to their significance:

> What has remained unknown in the world,
> is the mention of the history and stories of poets.
> *(Samarqandi, 2007: 22)*

This indicates that he had not encountered 'Awfi's *Lobāb al-albāb*, the collective work on poets and their work produced in the early thirteenth century that I have already discussed. Samarqandi's personal effort to correct what he saw as a critical lack occurred in the especially rich cultural world of the city of Herat during the second half of the fifteenth century. Presided over by the Timurid king Hosayn Bāyqarā (d. 1506) and his illustrious vizier 'Alishir Navā'i (d. 1501), this context was known for special investment in poetic circles (Subtelny, 1986). Samarqandi's work follows a traditional chronological structure, arranged by generations in the following order: an introduction that defines the significance of poets in human history and discusses a few famous Arabic poets from early Islamic history; seven chapters, each of which is named a level (*tabaqa*) and consists of between sixteen and twenty-one poets grouped together on the basis of generational contiguity; and a conclusion that describes six famous poets of the author's own day, followed by a lengthy notice on the king Hosayn Bāyqarā, who was also a poet.

Samarqandi's division of the work into seven levels and the further emphasis on seven contemporary figures (the six poets and the king) is not accidental. It reflects the general prevalence of the number seven as a mark of symmetry, such as in the case of the seven heavenly spheres of Ptolemaic cosmology and the division of the inhabited world into seven climes. Moreover, the placement of the king at the end gives the work a sense of progression toward improvement and higher status. The work is not strictly hierarchical, in that some of the poets on whom Samarqandi lavishes the greatest praise are to be found in seemingly random places within the overall narrative. The work does, nevertheless, convey the sense of being constructed like a building that has a base (the Arabic poets) and rises upward in the manner of the scheme of heavenly spheres.

Samarqandi's first order of business is to describe the significance of poets as a class based on rational observation as well as the citation of Islamic traditions. Echoing discussions like the ones I have highlighted in Section 2 of this Element, he emphasizes the human capacity for speech, through which God has distinguished the species from other animals:

> The animal gets fat from eating and drinking.
> The human being strengthens by means of the ear.
> *(6, citing Jalāloddin Rumi)*

The efficacy of speech is traced to eloquence, which is exemplified most significantly in poetry. This contains both the means to great pleasure and profound thought. He emphasizes the significance of poetry also through analogy with scriptural texts such as the Quran and revelations sent to other prophets, since both categories of speech are bearers of wisdom and eternal truths and can have transformative effects on human beings. Poetry's high status in all these fields is proven by noting that great kings of the pre-Islamic to the Islamic eras were either good poets themselves or at least connoisseurs of excellent poetry. Similarly on the religious front, poetry is attributed to some of Mohammad's companions as well as to admirable Muslim figures who have flourished in the centuries since the Prophet. All these proofs lead up to declaring virtuoso poets a human category that needs affirmation by compiling a work dedicated to them (Samarqandi, 2007, 5–18).

Samarqandi's specific notices on different poets vary greatly in terms of the level of detail he provides, whether with respect to individuals' lives or the contents of the poetic works. But the notices consistently focus on the interrelationship between a triad of elements highlighted in the preface: poetic virtuosity, political power, and Islamic religious excellence. To convey the flavor of Samarqandi's work, I will focus on his entries on Jalāloddin Rumi (d. 1274), Amir Khosrow of Delhi (d. 1338), and Shamsoddin Mohammad Hāfez

(d. 1390). These three men would make for prominent headings on any list of Persian poetry's greatest masters. All of them have been the subject of dozens of books; my brief comments here can do no justice whatsoever to their legacy. My object is to describe Samarqandi's entries on them, with emphasis on issues pertaining to interpersonal transactions.

3.1.1 Jalāloddin Rumi

Rumi's reputation as a preeminent poet bridges centuries, regions, and even languages (Lewis, 2000; Keshavarz, 1998). The high regard in which Rumi's poetry has been consistently held, from his own times to the modern period, is reflected in sumptuous manuscripts that survive to the present (see Figure 4). Samarqandi puts him in the fourth generation of his scheme for poets and describes him as one who was popular among all groups on account of revealing secrets of the hidden world in language:

> In that swelling sea, as the wave of nobility reached its height,
> beaches all around were showered with pearls of poetry.
> *(334)*

Rumi's father was a prominent scholar in Balkh (Afghanistan) at the time of Rumi's birth, but the family moved westward in his childhood. During the journey, in Nishapur, the child Rumi met Faridoddin 'Attar (d. 1221). The aging great Persian poet and Sufi author of the times recognized Rumi's resplendent future and gave him a copy of his work *Asrārnāmeh* (Book of Secrets). He told Rumi's father to expect momentous things of the boy. The family eventually settled in Konya (Turkey), where Rumi's father acquired a prominent position as scholar and preacher associated with the Rum Saljuq court. Rumi inherited this position upon his father's death.

Rumi's poetic output is connected to his meeting with Shams-e Tabriz. This enigmatic man arrived in Konya and made Rumi's world go topsy-turvy. At their very first meeting, Shams asked Rumi to explain religious exercises and what it means to have knowledge. When Rumi responded, "Sharia and following the Prophet's way," Shams said that that is all about external knowledge. Rumi then asked what more was there. Shams said that knowledge is the means that gets the seeker to what is being sought. He then recited the following verse from Sanā'i (d. 1131):

> Knowledge that does not take you beyond yourself,
> ignorance is much better than such knowledge.
> *(343)*

Figure 4 Beginning of Book Three of Jalāloddin Rumi's *Masnavi*. Iran, 1488–9. Ink, opaque watercolor, and gold on paper: 28.3 × 18.4 cm. Gift of Alexander Smith Cochran, 1913. The Metropolitan Museum of Art, New York. 13.228.12.

Rumi was amazed by this statement and gave up his mainstream ways as a religious scholar to become utterly devoted to Shams. When Shams left for Syria for two years, Rumi spent all his time pining after him: "Most ghazals that are written in Mawlānā's *Divan* were said while lamenting the separation from Shamsoddin. They say that there was a pillar in Mawlānā's house.

When he was drowning in the sea of love, he put his hand on the pillar and started spinning around it. He uttered lament-filled verses, which people then wrote down" (197). In this fashion, Rumi's desire for Shams was the source of both his great poetry and the ritual dance for which his community, the Mevlevis or Whirling Dervishes, has been known since the thirteenth century.

Shams's presence in Konya eventually led to jealousy on the part of Rumi's family and disciples. Samarqandi says that opinions varied on what happened to Shams but that speculating on this was frivolous. In addition to Shams, Rumi's poetry was inspired also by two other men: Salāhoddin Zarkub and Hosāmoddin Chalabi. These men are usually put chronologically later than Shams in Rumi's life. In Samarqandi's notice, they are mentioned first, without indicating any sense of succession (338). Rumi was a great name in his own day, and his poetic reputation kept increasing in later times.

The relationship pattern between Rumi and Shams in Samarqandi's account should remind us of the earlier discussion on Abu Sa'id Abil-Khayr's hagiographies. As there, poetry is a key ingredient for the two men to get connected as Sufis. But unlike Abu Sa'id, Shams quoting a verse in the first meeting has the effect of turning Rumi into a veritable fount of poetry. Samarqandi says that Rumi's *Divan* has 30,000 verses, while the number of verses in his *Masnavi* is estimated to be 47,000. It is also important in the narrative that Rumi gets an anointment from 'Attār as a child and that his transformation happens on the basis of Shams reciting a verse from Sanā'i. 'Attār and Sanā'i are both towering poets who preceded Rumi. The connection to them – one through physical contact and the gift of a book that transferred "secrets" to him, the other via poetic impression – places Rumi securely in Samarqandi's narration of the long history of Persian poetry.

3.1.2 Amir Khosrow

When it comes to his reputation as a poet, Amir Khosrow of Delhi ranks near to Rumi among those composing in Persian (Losensky and Sharma, 2011; Sharma, 2005). However, unlike Rumi, Khosrow was not the originator of a religious community whose significance went far beyond matters poetic. Instead, Khosrow was born in India of Turkish parentage and became a disciple to Nezāmoddin Awliyā (d. 1325), a Sufi master who has been regarded as a kind of patron saint of Delhi since the fourteenth century. According to Samarqandi, this great man held Khosrow in such high esteem that he would say: "On Resurrection day, I am hopeful that they will give me salvation due to the pain in the breast of this child of Turks" (418).

As with Rumi, Samarqandi puts Khosrow in the fourth generation of poets and connects him to the equally famous Moslehoddin Sa'di (d. ca. 1290) on account of having a similar ability to express complex matters through unpretentious poetic eloquence. He states also that Khosrow's voluminous poetic output had not been collected in one place during his life. This was a matter of consternation for one of his great admirers in the fifteenth century, the Timurid prince Bāysonghor (d. 1433). The prince expended much effort, which resulted in a collection containing 120,000 verses, although even this was less than what Khosrow himself had claimed to have composed in his lifetime.

Khosrow is especially famous for a series of five narrative poems known as the *Khamseh* (Quintet) done in imitation of the earlier *Khamseh* of Nezāmi Ganjavi (d. 1209). Nezāmi is another towering figure of Persian poetry, whose style and moralistic outlook were subjects of much emulation in later times. Bāysonghor's devotion to Khosrow's poetry was such that he got into a fight with another Timurid prince, his brother Ologh Bayg (d. 1449), who preferred Nezāmi. This led the two of them to sit through the long process of comparing the two very large *Khamsehs* (18,000 verses for Khosrow and 28,000 for Nezāmi) verse by verse, to prove whose was superior. Samarqandi does not tell us who won but comments: "If this partisanship had come about in current times, the decision of our critics, who are the jewelers of the market of excellence – may they live forever – would have shown the way to who is preferable and eliminated the error" (421–422). The statement leaves us hanging as to a judgment, but it was likely meant to defer the question to the views held by Hosayn Bāyqarā, the Timurid king, who was related to Bāysonghor and Ologh Bayg and presided over the poetry-infused environment in Herat during Samarqandi's own time.

Samarqandi remarks that, in addition to being a great poet, Khosrow was adept at music. In verses he cites, Khosrow says that a musician once asked him to judge whether music or poetry is better. Khosrow declared poetry to be of greater status because it does not need music, while the same is not true the other way around. These verses end with an analogy:

> Understand poetry to be a bride, music her ornaments.
> A beautiful bride with no ornaments is not at fault.
> *(Samarqandi, 2007: 429)*

Moments of repartee like this are a staple of Khosrow's poetry and reflect his embeddedness in the social life of his times. Courts feature prominently in the tales he tells, represented in the miniature paintings put in the expensive manuscripts of his works that were created in later centuries (see Figure 5).

Figure 5 "Shirin Entertains Khosrow, From a Copy of Amir Khosrow's *Khamseh*." Mohammad Hosayn Zarrin Qalam (scribe) and Manohar (artist), Lahore, Pakistan/Mughal India, 1597–8. Ink and paint on laid paper: 28.5 × 19 cm. The Walters Art Museum, Baltimore. W.624, Folio 51a.

The royal court was a metaphor for the world as such. It was the scene for the morality tales Khosrow constructed, which were relevant for all levels of society. His popularity in his own context in Delhi, as well as in centuries afterward throughout the Persian world, is predicated on his intimate familiarity with courts that championed literary production.

3.1.3 Shamsoddin Mohammad Hāfez

Hāfez of Shiraz is a grand figure in Persian literature, as well as in many other literary traditions through influence and translation (Brookshaw, 2019). His reputation as an ultimate master of ghazal poetry was well established by the time Samarqandi composed his work, about a century after the poet's death. His entry is placed in the fifth generation of Persian poets. It begins by indicating that Hāfez had become known by the title "tongue of the unseen" (*lesānol-ghayb*) because of the uniqueness of his way of putting thought into language, which seemed to stem from the world of hidden truths not available under ordinary human perception. Samarqandi points out that Hāfez's diction was simple and devoid of ornament, yet the ideas he expressed encapsulated wonders of meaning in pithy verses. Hāfez's genius was related to his mastery over the Quran (his chosen poetic sobriquet, Hāfez, indicates a person who knows the scripture by heart); his critique of worldly habits and hypocrisy; and the exaltation of Sufi-inspired poverty pervasive in his verse.

Samarqandi's account of Hāfez is divided equally between comment on his poetic excellence and on his relationships with royal figures. We are told that Hāfez composed a short praise poem for Sultan Ahmad Jalāyer (d. 1410) of Baghdad who was a great admirer of his poetry. When the conqueror Tamerlane (d. 1405) took Shiraz, he was already familiar with Hāfez's poetry. According to Samarqandi, he had taken exception to a very famous verse by Hāfez that begins one of his best-known ghazals. He had the poet brought to the court and queried as to whether he had said the following:

> If that Turk of Shiraz would take our heart in hand,
>> I would forfeit Samarkand and Bukhara for her/his black mole.

Tamerlane understood the verses as an insult to two of Central Asia's greatest cities, which he had conquered earlier and turned into glittering capitals. How could they be worth something as minor as a young person returning Hāfez's love? Hāfez's purported reply was that this was surely the poet's own error: it was precisely because of the kind of thoughtless generosity he was wont to disperse that he was in the terrible financial condition visible from his person at the time. This reply disarmed and charmed Tamerlane, indicating the great poet's ability to overcome a great king by his command of language (Samarqandi, 2007: 536–537). As detailed analyses have demonstrated, the verse about the Turk from Shiraz is likely connected to the politics of the court in Shiraz, to which Hāfez was attached, rather than anything to do with Tamerlane's conquest (Ingenito, 2018; Windfuhr, 1990).

One especially interesting aspect of Samarqandi's entry on Hāfez is that almost a third of it has nothing whatever to do with the poet himself. Instead, the author veers off to provide the story of Tamerlane subduing Sultan Ahmad Jalāyer with the help of his allies in the Iran-Iraq region. The story of Tamerlane vanquishing Ahmad does, however, relate to the use of poetry and is helpful for understanding Hāfez's place in the world. Samarqandi writes that when Ahmad was defying Tamerlane, one of his actions was to send the conqueror some verses of his own composition:

> Why should we stoop our neck to the dictates of time?
> Why should we take the trouble for every small skirmish?
> Rivers and mountains, we cross and roam.
> Like Simurgh, we flap wings over land and water.
> We step on, roaming around, as we wish,
>   endeavoring forth, like true men.
>
> *(539)*

When he got the message, Tamerlane fretted that he was not a poet himself to be able to respond in kind, although he hoped that someone in his family may be able to do it. The matter went to Tamerlane's son Amirānshāh (d. 1394) and his son (Tamerlane's grandson) Khalil Soltān (d. 1411). This then led to verses that were sent to Ahmad Jalāyer as a response:

> Stoop your neck, bow to the times.
> This great affair is no small matter.
> How can you go to Qāf Mountain like the Simorgh,
>   when you are a little finch, feather and wing plucked.
> Expel impossible missions from your mind,
>   so a hundred thousand heads don't roll for the sake of your head.
>
> *(540)*

Hearing this response, Ahmad understood that he had no chance. He abandoned Baghdad to Tamerlane and escaped to Anatolia

In Samarqandi's work, it is quite common to find poetic altercations between military rivals placed within entries that are ostensibly about poets. I believe we can see this pattern as a symptom of poetry's use as a political tool. Poetic words could be made into weapons and be a means with which to carry out internecine rivalries. Poets such as Hāfez were embedded within this world as mouthpieces for hire and as companions enlivening courtly environments. To reach high status in this situation required poetic talent and the ability to parlay it in discourse, as we see in the story of the supposed meeting between Tamerlane and Hāfez.

Samarqandi's ultimate subject in his *Tazkeratosh-sho'arā* was not the collectivity of poets but poetry itself, as an art and an instrument that got actualized through words put together by the great poets. In a frame larger than Samarqandi's work, the materialization of this poetry extended to all media, including textiles such as the Ardabil carpets. These are two of the most famous Persian carpets ever produced and the first thought to have a date (946/1539–40). On one of them, right above the date and signature of the maker, there is a verse from Hāfez (see Figure 6):

> There is no haven for me in this world save your abode.
> There is nowhere to place my head except here.

In presenting Samarqandi's notices on Rumi, Khosrow, and Hāfez very briefly, I have had reason to invoke the names of four other stalwarts who were these poets' predecessors: 'Attār, Sanā'i, Sa'di, and Nezāmi. Taken together, the seven names act like nodes sprouting lines in an intensively connected web of poetic production spread throughout Samarqandi's narrative. While his framework is pegged to chronology in the form of the seven generations, references inside his entries crisscross across time, invoking connections between poets and styles old and new, all related to other matters such as politics and religion. The resulting work is a tapestry-like cultural history whose base is the art of composing verses in Persian.

3.2 Social Hierarchy

Tohfeh-ye Sāmi, the second biographical dictionary I present in this section, was composed by someone who could have been king. Sām Mirzā Safavi (d. 1567) was a son of Esmā'il I, who founded the Safavid dynasty in Iran in 1501. We have already met Sām Mirzā's brother Tahmāsp, the second king in the dynasty, who instituted the scheme that benefited Awhadi as a child growing up as an orphan. Sām Mirzā's political career included governorships of various provinces under his brother, although this was always a precarious condition to be in because kings in the Persian world saw their brothers as potential rivals. He eventually perished in 1567 as the result of an earthquake while imprisoned in Qahqaheh castle (northwest Iran), a venue known to house political detainees (Ambraseys and Melville, 1982: 49). The work's modern editor estimates that it was composed circa 1550–60, in the period immediately before the author was incarcerated (Safavi, 2005: xix).

Sām Mirzā begins the work by describing the significance of speech and poetry customary for the genre in which he was writing: "Poetry is the invaluable gem of the mine of being, the highest star in the desired heaven" (3). Like Samarqandi's work, *Tohfeh-ye Sāmi* has seven parts. However, the divisions are based on social hierarchy rather than chronology, indicating a different metaphorical deployment of the seven-fold structure of the cosmos. They proceed as follows:

Figure 6 Detail with verse from Hāfez on carpet. Ardabil carpet. Maqsud
Kāshāni, Iran (possibly Tabriz), 1539-40. Wool knotted pile on silk plain weave
foundation: 718.82 × 400.05 cm (full carpet). Gift of J. Paul Getty. Los Angeles
County Museum of Art, 53.50.2. Digital Image © 2020 Museum Associates/
LACMA. Licensed by Art Resource, NY.

1. Accounts of Shāh Esmāʿil (author's royal father), his children, and kings
   contemporary to him;
2. Sayyeds and religious scholars;
3. Viziers and other "masters of the pen";
4. Other people worthy of respect who wrote poetry, although they were not
   poets;
5. Established poets;
6. Turks who were poets;
7. Ordinary people.

What is striking here is, of course, that in a book devoted to poets and poetry,
the first four chapters are explicitly on people whose primary identities lie in
fields other than poetry. As a kind of chronicle fixated on poetry, the work
functions as a declaration of jurisdiction over the poetic domain in conjunction
with other territorial claims put forth by the dynasty of which Sām Mirzā was

a member. The author's choice can then be pegged to his own firm placement within the political milieu.

Indexing the work to a state headed by his father and brother casts it as a document of political fidelity. To further avoid any confusion in this regard, a statement of warning precedes the notices:

> During the process of describing the conditions of this prosperous class, if mention is sometimes made of those who are enemies of [the correct] religion and state ... this neither corrupts religion nor sullies the state. As said in the noble Quran, "There is nothing wet or dry except that it is in the eloquent Book." ... The purpose behind narrating the story of this group is history and not inclusion among those who are favored. (4–5)

Sām Mirzā's organization has the effect too of creating a distinction between poetry as a widespread practice and the identity of being a professional poet. His notices in the first four chapters do consistently focus on individuals who composed poetry, who are described together with examples of their output. The key is that these peoples' primary identities were as something other than poets. People included in chapters five through seven, in comparison, are poets proper, because they have distinguished themselves in this category in society.

The fifth chapter is the work's core, comprising more than half of its total length. Of the 712 entries included in the published edition, 369 are in the fifth chapter, consisting of poets whose lives are placed in the approximate period 1450–1560. Within all chapters, entries are arranged according to social and poetic stature rather than chronology or alphabetical order. To provide further sense of Sām Mirzā's work, I will focus on his entry on a poet named 'Abdollāh Hātefi (d. 1521).

The word *hātef* means a voice heard when the speaker is not visible to the hearer. It is commonly used to indicate supernatural interventions by God or other beings who are not physically visible. (In modern Arabic, *hātef* is a word for the telephone.) At the beginning of the sixteenth century, when the Persian world was undergoing massive political changes with the establishment of new dynasties, a poet with the pen name Hātefi ("of the *hātef*"), whose proper name was 'Abdollāh, was among the most celebrated living exemplars of his craft. The pen name indicates his conceit to be the mouthpiece of the unseen realm. This Hātefi is the third entry in the fifth chapter of Sām Mirzā's work, indicating the very high regard in which he was held. Sām Mirzā's description of Hātefi's work is especially useful because it shows him to us placed within a web of relationships to his predecessors and contemporaries.

The account begins by noting that Hātefi was the son of a sister of 'Abdorrahmān Jāmi (d. 1491). Resident in Herat, Jāmi was a towering literary and religious figure of his time. He is the first entry in Sām Mirzā's fifth chapter. In hindsight, Jāmi has been regarded by some as the last of the great classical Persian poets (d'Hubert and Papas, 2019). Sām Mirzā presents Hātefi as Jāmi's poetic heir, his work being intertwined with that of his venerated elder relative in multiple ways.

Sām Mirzā writes that when Hātefi got the urge to write a quintet (*khamseh*) on the well-established pattern, he sought Jāmi's advice. Jāmi told him that if he could respond to certain verses from Ferdowsi's *Shāhnāmeh* (which he provided) then that would mean that he had the capacity to do the quintet. Hātefi composed a response, which Jāmi liked and approved, even though these verses were not of the same level as Ferdowsi's originals. Further in the process, Hātefi asked Jāmi to provide the beginning verses to *Layli va Majnun*, one of the five poems in the quintet. Jāmi obliged and Hātefi used these as the starter for the rest of the composition (159–161).

Hātefi's other works included the *Haft manzar* (Seven Scenes) done in emulation of Nezāmi's celebrated *Haft payker* (Seven Beauties or Paintings). This became a much celebrated work that was copied in expensive manuscripts with illustrations, such as one made for the court of 'Abdol-'Aziz Khan Uzbek (d. 1539) in Bukhara (see Figure 7). The Uzbeks were the Safavids' bitter rivals. The fact that we can find Hātefi honored on both sides of the political divide tells us that celebrity in the poetic field transcended political allegiances. Hātefi was famous also for his *Temornāmeh* (Book of Tamerlane), written in the vein of similar works on Alexander, the paradigmatic conqueror in Persian lore and literature (Bernardini, 2003). Between these works, Hātefi was the renowned poet who connected the tradition of Persian poetry's accepted classics to great political and literary figures of his own day (161–163).

In addition to poetic issues, Sām Mirzā provides information on Hātefi's personal circumstances. He is said to have lived in a small town named Khargerd-e Jām (Iran, near Afghanistan border) where he was the caretaker of the mausoleum of Shāh Qāsem-e Anvār (d. 1433), himself a much celebrated poet and Sufi master in earlier times. Sām Mirzā states that when his father, Shāh Esmā'il, conquered this region, he made a point of visiting Khargerd-e Jām in order to pay homage to the grave of Qāsem-e Anvār. There he met Hātefi, had a meal with him, and asked him to recite some of his verses. Greatly pleased by what he heard, Esmā'il then appointed him to produce a versified account of his conquests. Hātefi had composed 1,000 verses for this commission by the time he died. He was buried in the same garden where he had spent most of his life (163–164).

Sām Mirzā's *Tohfeh-ye Sāmi* provides us a view of poetry from the vantage point of people intensively invested in poetry but without regarding this as

Figure 7 Painting in a copy of Hātefi's *Haft manzar*. Mir ʿAli Heravi (scribe) and Shaykhzādeh (artist), Bukhara, Uzbekistan, 1538. Opaque watercolor, ink, and gold on paper: 26.2 × 16.8 cm. Freer Gallery of Art, Smithsonian Institution, Washington, DC, Purchase – Charles Lang Freer Endowment. F1956.14, Folio 78r.

a vocation. His discussion of poets proper is preceded by four chapters on nonpoets, although he does then give the honor of place to those celebrated as poets. The entry on Hātefi connects to Jāmi, Nezāmi, and Qāsem-e Anvār as earlier poets and to Shāh Esmāʿil as someone who was a poet himself and patronized them as a class when he was king. At the end of the work, Sām Mirzā cites some of his own compositions, which indicate a competent but poor talent. His work shows him to be a skilled amateur admirer of good poetry rather than one who could pretend to be a master himself (377–380). From the work, we can see the social and political significance of poetic discourse and the heavily interconnected nature of poetic production, in Sām Mirzā's immediate context and across the centuries.

3.3 Gender Trouble

The last work I consider in this section is distinguished by the fact that it is devoted entirely to female poets. Fakhri-Heravi's *Javāherol-'ajā'eb* (Wondrous Gems) is thought to be the first work of its kind, although women do feature occasionally in earlier works that are populated mostly by men. This work's author was born and raised in Herat and was a member of the same circles in which Hātefi made his name. His deep interest in poetry is reflected in the fact that, while in Herat, he translated (and expanded) from Chaghatay Turkish into Persian a work on poets entitled *Majāleson-nafā'es* by the eminent vizier and poet 'Alishir Navā'i (Navā'i, 1945). In the *Javāherol-'ajā'eb*, he says that he left Herat for India (likely around 1540) with the intention of going on the hajj. This led him to the court of the rulers of Sind (now Pakistan), the same region where 'Awfi had composed his *Lobābol-albāb* more than three centuries earlier.

The *Javāherol-'ajā'eb* exists in two versions that have different prefaces. The first version is dedicated to Hāji Baygom, a royal lady at the court in Sind, and was composed around 1555 (70). The author later moved further eastward, to the Mughal court in Agra under Akbar. The second version of the work is dedicated to Māham Angeh, Akbar's foster mother, who held great power during the early years of his rule as a minor (30–35, 114–115). In a painting depicting Akbar as a boy emperor, she appears at the center of the courtly stage (see Figure 8).

Fakhri writes in his preface that one day, after coming back from the court in Sind, he began browsing the poetry in the *Tohfatol-habib*, an anthology of ghazals imitated between poets he had put together earlier while in Herat. His eyes fell on a poem by the lady Mehri composed as a response to an earlier one by Hāfez. The poem was so good that many people thought that it was one by Hāfez himself. This led him to think that he should put together a collection of "that which has become apparent in the garment of poetry by women, since it is quite amazing" (116). This instinct resulted is a collection of notices on thirty-one women, presented in an order that mixes status and chronology.

Figure 8 Festivities at the marriage Of Bāqi Mohammad Khan, son of Māham
Angeh. At Akbar's court in 1561. In a copy of Abol-Fazl's *Akbarnāmeh*.
Outline by La'l, painting by Sanwala, India, 1590–5. Opaque watercolor and
gold on paper: 33 × 20 cm. Victoria and Albert Museum, London. IS.2:9-1896.

The *Javāherol-'ajā'eb* proceeds as follows: Del-ārām (a beloved of the pre-
Islamic Persian king Bahrām Gur); 'Āesheh and Fātemeh (wife and daughter,
respectively, to the Prophet Mohammad); Zolaykhā (the woman who tempts the

prophet Joseph in the Bible and the Quran and was a primary character in numerous Persian verse compositions); seven female poets from the Saljuq, Ilkhan, Enju, Jalāyer, and early Timurid periods (ca. 1100–1450); and twenty women who had lived in Central Asia and Iran in recent times (ca. 1450 to 1550). India is conspicuously absent from the collection, likely because the author had arrived there quite recently. The work also conveys the sense of the author presenting women poets from Iran and Central Asia to the distinguished Indian ladies to whom his work is dedicated.

The sequencing of Fakhri's work is quite eclectic, the first four women situated in places and times greatly removed from the last twenty-seven. It seems to me that the four act as anchors of proper womanhood to create a base pattern. This is then exemplified in the stories of those who can be documented from recent memory.

Fakhri identifies the legendary king Bahrām Gur and Del-ārām as originators of Persian poetry. Poetry as a kind of linguistic practice came about when Bahrām said something and Del-ārām responded in the same rhyme and meter, giving him the idea that this was a good game. Persian poetry is thus born betwixt the two genders. This is significant in part because Persian does not have grammatical gender, so the same pronoun applies to 'she', 'he', and 'it'. Placing the first verse ever enunciated as bifurcated between a woman and a man inscribes gender into language above grammatical neutrality.

Predictably, 'Āesheh and Fātemeh anchor poetry in Islamic terms. The first recites a verse to the Prophet in the context of their married life, and the second says one of lament at his death. Both of these are in Arabic. Zolaykhā is a carrier of the notion of uncontrolled passion for another person. The more extended version of Fakhri's notice on her has, first, a verse on love in Arabic she says to Joseph; second, the work cites verses by Jāmi and Helāli (d. 1529) in Persian, excerpted from larger works of these two recent great models, in which she is the speaker (119–120). This means that Zolaykhā is being celebrated as a poet not because of what she produced. Rather, words from later male poets who portray her as one of the great lovers of all time are used to represent her voice and emotions.

One key to Fakhri's work is that his account of women insists that gender matters. Del-ārām and Zolaykhā are important for this because they address themselves to men as desiring women. As paradigmatic wife and daughter, 'Āesheh and Fātemeh serve a similar function in the field of kinship. The gender dynamic is further dramatized in instances where more recent female poets utilize repartee to assert their rights as desiring subjects fully able to deploy poetic language. This occurs in a world shown to be dominated by men. I will provide details for two entries relevant to this observation: first, one on the aforementioned lady Mehri, whose work started the author on the path of composing the work; and second, one on a woman named Bijeh, who is shown to compete with the great poet and religious authority 'Abdorrahmān Jāmi.

Fakhri says that Mehri was a companion to Gowhar Shād Baygom (d. 1457), powerful wife of Tamerlane's successor Shāhrokh Mirzā (d. 1447) and mother of the princes Bāysonghor and Ologh Bayg (mentioned earlier) who got into a fight about the poetry of Amir Khosrow. This queen was a major patron of architecture and the arts and was executed at the age of eighty for fear she would exercise her influence among rivals in the Timurid family (Manz, 2007: 257–264).

Fakhri says that Mehri was extremely beautiful but was married to an old man whom she did not like. She and her husband as a couple are shown to perform their misgivings about each other in public via poetic altercations. One day when she was with Gowhar Shād, the queen saw her old husband from afar and asked him to come over. As he ambled along slowly, the queen asked Mehri to compose something about him on the spot. She responded with the following verses:

> I have no passion left for you,
>> nothing remains of a loving heart and faithfulness.
> Just as to you, from weakness and old age,
>> there remains no capacity to lift your feet.
>
> *(125)*

Rather than her husband, Mehri was inclined to one of Gowhar Shād's nephews. On Eid, she went to visit him to offer felicitations. As she was with the prince in the tower of the fort of Herat, her husband walked by and the prince pointed him out to her. She responded with irony:

> I rose to my moon at the top of a tower.
> Yes, wise one, have a look at my fortunate rising star!

During springtime one year, Mehri joined the whole city in enjoying the sights outside. She saw an old man who had fallen hopelessly in love with her and was staring at her in a disheveled state. She had him brought over and asked after him. He responded, "What is utterly evident has no need to be explained." She smiled and said the following quatrain:

> God, what water and clay make up my constitution,
>> all my desire is for the beloveds of Chigil.
> If my inclination had been toward the elderly,
>> what complaint would I have of the old, feeble one.
>
> *(126)*

Chigil was a place nearby famous for being the home of beautiful people.

Fakhri's stories about Mehri have a highly staged quality, such that one thinks one is seeing not an actual person but a case where reports have been streamlined to create a literary character usable for particular ends. In the case of Mehri, the stories are especially focused on dichotomies like female and male, youth and old age, beauty and ugliness. In all of them, she is fixed to being a beautiful young woman with the gift of poetry and wit whom life has handed a lemon in the form of an old husband. What we learn from the entry is not the life of a person, but performative possibilities pertaining to these dichotomies that prevailed within Persian literary idioms.

Fakhri's entry on Bijeh is quite different from that for Mehri. She is described as being learned and witty rather than beautiful, and she competes with men with these qualities rather than lamenting her lot in life. She is said to have been especially adept at astronomy, with scholarly credentials high enough for her to be a desired presence in courts. Fakhri states that, to assert her ambition, she emulated 'Abdorrahmān Jāmi, constructing a public bath, school, and mosque just like he had done. When the mosque was complete, she invited Herat's religious elite to come and pray there. Jāmi refused, which incensed her: "'Whatever he has constructed, I have too. All the virtues he has, I do too. He writes poetry, so do I. What does he have that I do not?' Mollā [Jāmi] said, 'We have a thing that she does not.' She responded, 'We too have a thing that he does not – moreover, he is the one who needs us'" (131). Jāmi liked this response very much and decided to be her guest.

The only poetry from Bijeh is a verse she said at the death of her husband:

> My fortune's star, the sky was radiant from him.
> See, o moon, separated from you now, he is under the earth.
>
> *(131)*

In this verse too, Bijeh contrasts sharply with Mehri. The husband's death is a great loss rather than him being a burden while alive.

In Fakhri's work, the poets' gender becomes prominent when they are shown in an amorous or antagonistic relationship with men. When this is not the case, it is impossible to tell the difference between male and female poets, since neither the pronouns nor the verbal endings are gendered in Persian. Moreover, whoever takes up the pen to compose poetry speaks in a specific dialect with clear expectations regarding conventions, precedents, and so on. This has the effect of occluding gender. From a work like that of Fakhri, we get a direct sense of play pertaining to gender, albeit in a highly stylized form.

3.4 Poetic Lives

The market in Persian poetry we see in works from the Middle Ages is an overwhelmingly male domain. In this, the materials match most of the rest of what is available to us to tell the story of the Persian world. This makes it all the more important to include documents such as Fakhri's *Javāherol-'ajā'eb* in an assessment of the topic. This short compilation, which reports on only thirty-one poets, is a crucially significant counterpart to works that tell of hundreds and even thousands of male poets because it illuminates the gap between texts and society.

As we have seen, excelling in the craft of writing poetry required training, access to networks of mentors and patrons, ability to show one's wares in public to become a part of political transactions, the possibility of travel (as evident from the lives of all those who made their way from Iran and Central Asia to India), and membership in the convivial yet competitive gatherings where poetry was recited and reputations were established. The social underpinnings of all these processes overwhelmingly privileged men as prototypical candidates for membership. Women were exceptional participants, and notices on them are more exceptional still because of the fact of limited representation in the literary record.

Male-centeredness is an issue that extends to eroticism within the Persian poetic world as well. While the pronouns in Persian are neutral, both the lover and the beloved in the fiction underlying the poetic dialect in Persian are presumed male by convention, especially in the exceedingly popular ghazal form. This means that, irrespective of whether the speaking poet is male or female, s/he takes up the posture of an adult male whose gaze is addressed to a younger, usually prepubescent male person. To what degree this convention translated to the social world is a complex question, in that homosexuality and pederasty were legally inadmissible in the codes that governed societies in the Persian world.

However, male-to-male erotic relationships were widely tolerated, with differentiated positions ascribed to older male lovers and younger male beloveds. In poetic erotic mapping of the human body, the androgynous figure, presumed to be male, comes across as the main object (Rāmi, 1947). In Sufi contexts, where poetry provided the key script to create relationships between masters and disciples, the norm was for both to be male. When present, female disciples or masters had to treat erotic aspects of relationships in metaphorical rather than material ways (Bashir, 2011: 109–115, 135–154).

The primacy of the social highlighted by considering women's restricted access to poetry and other spheres of life helps us appreciate marginality as a general concern when reading the sources and constructing the picture of the market in poetry in the Persian world. The literary corpus available to us is primarily of elite origins, because literacy was a restricted good. Moreover, literary materials that ended up being preserved for the long run come from classes that had more economic resources. For male poets represented in dictionaries of poets, we certainly have stories where people born in underprivileged circumstances were successful. In this vein, poetry could be a means for upward social mobility at least for some, actualized on the basis of a combination of innate ability and fortuitous accidents. Still, poetry as a profession was akin to other prestigious paths, available mostly to individuals born into advantageous social situations. While there is ample incidental indication that poetic practice permeated all levels of society, most of the evidence we have to tell the story comes from male political, socioeconomic, and religious elites.

4 Complex Poetic Instruments

My primary aim in this Element is not to narrate the history of Persian poetry but to see poetic production and consumption as a kind of flow that helps us understand society as such. To this end, in this last section, I would like to introduce a number of cases that highlight the place of poetry in materials that are not focused on poetry as such. Calling these cases complex poetic instruments refers to the fact that investment in complexity was a part of the intention of those who created the materials. Moreover, "consumption" here is an activity we can assign equally to those who produced poetry and those who heard and utilized it. From these instances, we see how poetry permeated most aspects of societal and discursive reproduction in the Persian world during the Middle Ages.

As sections on evaluation of poetry and the lives of poets have shown, creating poetry required practitioners to have extensive familiarity with a tradition stretching over centuries. Whatever one composed was inherently in dialogue with what had come before. In fact, excelling in Persian poetry required exceptional skill precisely because compositions had to stay within narrow confines of defined meters, rhymes, and allegorical conventions. The more intertextual one could make one's work – a process understood under the general notion of welcoming a past poet – the more one was regarded as an exceptional poet. The trick of genius was to create novel and striking meanings out of stories and fictional frames that were hackneyed in terms of their basics. All a versifier could do was to parrot the basics. A true poet took the same baselines and created a symphony that included citations to predecessors and opened new vistas for the listener (Lewis, 2019; Losensky, 1998b: 100–114; Zipoli, 1993).

The ingenuity presumed to be at the heart of Persian poetic tradition made it an instrument usable in contexts beyond poetic recital on its own. Here I go through four examples in quick succession to help us see the effects of poetry being a thing of value in the Persian world as both practice and product. The contexts I have chosen are: translation, as it is represented in an early sixteenth-century Persian transformation of a work from Chaghatay Turkish in India; history, as seen in hyperbolic performances from sixteenth-century Iran; a memoir infused with poetic nostalgia written in Central Asia in the middle of the sixteenth century; and three composite works created, respectively, in Anatolia, Iran, and India between the fourteenth and the seventeenth centuries.

4.1 Translation

I began the Element by referring to a translator who called a worthy verse the equivalent of a pearl attached to the king's ear. In this section, I go back to this work. Zayn Khān Khwāfi's *Tabaqāt-e Bāborī* is billed as a partial translation of a work usually known under the name *Bābornāmeh*, a personal memoir of Bābor, the Central Asian Timurid prince who became the first Mughal emperor in India. Khwāfi was a bureaucrat and man of letters who accompanied Bābor from Kabul to India in 1525 CE. Although the work is based on Bābor's memoir and follows its narrative order, it is not a straightforward translation. Shaykh Zayn was present at the events he describes spanning the period 1525–7, and his work adds to Bābor's representations. He also transforms an idiosyncratic first-person account by a royal figure into a more generically proper "chronicle" viable as a professional representation of the past. The insertion of additional Persian verses is essential to his objectives.

The celebrity of Bābor's original memoir is based on the author's significance as a historical actor and the narrative's seemingly frank tone that has been contrasted with the florid prose common for materials from this period (Dale, 2004). Bābor's account has a temporal scheme: it is arranged chronologically in the sequence of hijri years, and he claims that he is telling things as they happened. But the work differs from a usual chronicle in that Bābor himself is the main subject of his work. Customarily, a chronicle has as its subject a king, dynasty, or locality and is penned by a member of the literati whose own subject position is to stand outside of the story as a raconteur or observer. Authors do certainly bring themselves into the narratives, but, unlike in the case of Bābor, professional chroniclers' works are not the stories of their own lives.

Khwāfi's job in the *Tabaqāt-i Bābori* was to translate Bābor's narrative in two ways: one, he converted it from Chaghatay Turkish to Persian; and two, he attempted to make it into a chronicle rather than a royal autobiography. As we might say it today, the latter move amounts to putting Bābor's words in quotation marks as direct citations, surrounded by Khwāfi's chronicler's voice that provides context for understanding Bābor. The result is an incongruous narrative since it is a chronicle that is, uncharacteristically, reliant on a single witness as its source. But it is this very incongruity that affords us the chance to see history in the making in the early sixteenth century.

Khwāfi's augmentation of Bābor's narrative includes additional points of information as well as rhetorical embellishment (it omits material from the original as well). Poetry within the narrative is a kind of time regulator that allows the author to perform the braiding of the past, the present, and the future. Three elements pertaining to time relate to poetic insertions: atemporality or cosmic motion (a realm beyond time that acts as a kind of framing of time); scalable temporalities (the way descriptions of events in the depicted past are rendered meaningful through reference to timelines and to past and future events); and phenomenality (the sense of being in a place at a time).

In comparison with the straightforward yearly organization of Bābor's original, Khwāfi's work includes an effort to draw correlations between events he describes and ideologically significant temporal frames. This is done mostly through verse, with the other major method being citations of Quranic verses or easily recognizable Hadith, provided in Arabic.

The work begins with Bābor's army setting out from Kabul, an occasion that in Bābor's original is noted by its hijri date and the observation that the sun was in the constellation Sagittarius. Khwāfi conveys this data identically but then dramatizes the event by positing Bābor as the sun and his archers as an army in the heavens imitating the image of the zodiac sign. This turns Bābor's actions into cosmic movement:

> Sinking into Pisces, rising upon the moon.
> The lance's tip, the court's dome.
> What a splendid court it was that, like the sun,
>   extended its ropes from the east to the west.
> What a splendid lance that, like the banner of faith,
>   reached the uppermost heaven with its great height.
> As the heaven raised victory's banner,
>   it conjured up victory's signs.
> Fate conveyed to him the news of his good fortune:
> "Aid from God, and a near victory."
>   *(3a; last line quoted from Quran 61:13)*

The text repeats the juxtaposition, usually in verse, between Bābor and the sun at numerous critical junctures in which Bābor's actions and ambitions require justification. Allusions to the constancy and inevitable nature of the movement of astrological bodies work to naturalize Bābor's actions as part of a cosmic cycle.

The second temporal framing accomplished through poetry is when Khwāfi contextualizes Bābor's actions with respect to human pasts. A prominent case for this is his account of Bābor's victory at Panipat (India) in 1526, which he compares to Tamerlane's earlier conquest of Delhi in 1398 in an extensive section that mixes prose and poetry. The section ends with a long verse citation beginning with the following:

> I do not say that the king was mightier,
>   than the Lord of the Conjunction, the domain's protector.
> I do not say that, compared to Timur's grandeur,
>   Bābor's glory was greater.
> But I do ask a question of the knowledgeable:
> In the strength of manliness and warfare,
>   is not the brave-natured one who, with ten thousand,
>   took on a hundred thousand opponents
>   greater than the one who fought with a million
>   of orderly troops with an early advantage?
>
> *(55b)*

Khwāfi's ultimate judgment regarding the matter is that Bābor's victory was greater because he received divine help rather than relying on military might alone.

It is no surprise that a court chronicler such as Khwāfi makes comparisons between Bābor and the sun and Tamerlane. For Muslim kings, the cast is easily extended to others, such as Mohammad, 'Ali, heroes from the *Shāhnāmeh*, and earlier kings. In the case of Indian works, figures from Hindu mythology were brought to bear on ethical and political advice (Truschke, 2020). Such comparisons put the lives of protagonist royal figure into larger patterns of time. For astral bodies, the king's actions become part of natural cycles with plotted pasts and futures. For past human exemplars, the trajectories of known stories justify and legitimize the particular events that are being related and project illustrious futures. Poetry is the critical glue that allows articulating the connections.

The third important theme is that poetry has to be introduced whenever Khwāfi describes states of heightened sensory appreciation or episodes involving strong emotional resonances. While poetry was generally the carrier of these aspects of experience in this context, here it is put in service of a historical narrative. Some examples can help explain what I mean.

First, we go back to the story of Bābor and his entourage spending a night on the barge with which I began this Element. Bābor's original describes the circumstances that led to the event and tells about the party whiling away the nighttime composing poetry. Khwāfī adds a description of the night that includes the following verses:

> The pleasing night, like the dawn of life,
> a goad to joy, like the time of one's youth.
> Taking rest from the movement of fish and fowl,
> drawing up the march of events in its skirts,
> the night as thief robs the malcontent of their sleep,
> it silences the bells of those who ring bells.
> In this garden, a palace filled with spectacles,
> there remained no falcon save the stars' bright eyes.
>
> *(10b)*

This description conveys a sense of the night as it might be experienced by a small company, isolated from the normal course of life. The situation's tranquility is conveyed through the absence of the normal and the metaphorization of things that become visible at night alone.

A second example is when the king gives himself up to drink at one point:

> His diver-like heart tossing in the waves of the sea of wine,
> pushed and pulled the rope attached to the intellect.
> A king whose conquered territory was the whole world,
> was himself conquered by a bit of liquid in the matter of a moment.
>
> *(61b–62a)*

Here Bābor's drunken state is evoked through metaphors, with the addition of irony that contrasts human fragility with the ability to perform great deeds.

> The last example is the description of a garden built by Bābor in India:
> Like the garden of Iram in its beauty and pleasantness.
> The envy of the sacred house for its light and purity.
> Its open spaces like the courtyard of the sublime paradise.
> Its atmosphere like the breaths of the faithful spirit.
> Sweet basil and hyacinth in each other's embrace.
> The rose and the jasmine swaying side by side.
> Its buildings all like new inventions,
> their four walls balanced finely like a quatrain's lines.
>
> *(84b)*

The extended description in verse comes after a detailed prose section that explains the construction of the garden. The verses convey, hyperbolically, a sense of being in the garden by comparing it to other places and natural sights presumably experienced by the reader. The reference to a quatrain reflects the way awareness of the relationship between aesthetics and poetic structures seeps into metaphorical constructions at a general level.

These examples convey a sensory appreciation of the world that is being described in the text. This is a significant feature of the text as a whole, since the author's purpose is not simply to relate "what happened" in a bare-bones fashion but to convey a sense of the past, relying on conventions shared with the reader. Bābor's own text makes for instructive contrast in this regard, since it is focused solely on his own person rather than being concerned with participation in shared social and aesthetic paradigms encoded into literary forms.

These examples help us see the significance of poetry in creating a sense of history. The three narrative elements I have highlighted – cosmic time, earthly temporality, and phenomenality – combine to project a picture that, through its embellishments, is far more complex in the translation than the original. Cosmic time marks a kind of absolute point that transcends the ephemeral and the changeable and is the carrier of the narrative's prescriptive ethical and moral dimension. In contrast, earthly temporality involves multiple time scales that frame the description of events and lives and is the bearer of diachronic ideas, such as causality, development, and cyclicity. And phenomenality encompasses affective issues, such as experience and aesthetics. Inserting poetic interjections is Khwāfi's means of translating the work into not just another language but the form expected of the chronicle in the context.

4.2 History

About the time Khwāfi was composing his work in India, the poet Qāsemi Gonābādi was writing a chronicle in verse to present the story of Shāh Esmāʻil in Iran. As we saw in Sām Mirzā's entry on the poet Hātefi, Esmāʻil was keen on both poetry and the celebration of his conquests. He was himself a poet too, although in Turkish, in which literary context he holds an important place (Csirkés, 2019; Gallagher, 2018). His commission to Hātefi did not conclude properly because of the poet's death. The burden then fell to Qāsemi Gonābādi, who saw himself as a follower of Hātefi. He composed the *Shāh Esmāʻil-nāmeh* under the patronage of Esmāʻil's son Tahmāsp. The work was completed in 1533, a decade after the death of its subject.

Gonābādi's work is a consummate representation of the interdependence between kings and poets that I have discussed earlier. In a section that comments on the connection between speech and royal action, he addresses his erstwhile patron, the king whose exploits are the work's subject, in the following way:

> Of merchandise of speech, you are the buyer.
> Just as you are a Sanjar, I am Anvari.
> Your good name I sketch, after this,

on pages of time's passage.
Khezr never gave Alexander the water;
    but elixir of everlasting life I give you in this text ...
Many a palace and portal raised high,
    the higher sphere has thrown back to ground.
The building in speech I create suffers no harm
    from the primordial sphere.

(165)

Further in the work, he echoes a sentiment that we encountered in 'Aruzi's work composed nearly 500 years earlier:

If it weren't for poetry,
    of kings no sign nor trace would remain in the world.
When Anvari rendered fresh poetry's form,
    he made the world echo with Sanjar's fame.
Sweet-spoken Nezāmi's poems bring Alexander alive,
    give Parviz his name.
If Hātefi didn't make magic,
    creating splendid pieces of poetic dress,
    if he didn't string pearls portraying Timur,
    the world's ears wouldn't overflow with him.
In your time, this is what it is like for me:
    your name I strike on coins of speech ...
If the name of Jam and Kāyqubād remains
    from the poetry of noble Ferdowsi,
    this work will remain, it is hoped,
    like an image celebrating your name.

(170–171)

Gonābādi's deployment of the poet–king relationship is true to the old form, the thing to note being that there is nothing subliminal about this whatsoever. In poetry, the poet forthrightly claims his due, reminding the king that his work is a necessity and not a mere embellishment. The direct address we see here indicates how central poetry was to discourse aimed at legitimizing political power in the Persian world during the Middle Ages. As such, it was an exceedingly valuable commodity created by craftspeople in high demand (Sharlet, 2011).

I would like to add to the picture by considering a chronicle that deploys poetry in an unusual way. Mahmud Natanzi's chronicle entitled *Noqāvatol-āsār fi zekrol-akhyār* (The Best Traces Remembering Those Gone By) was completed in 1598 in Iran, about half a century after Gonābādi. This lengthy work covers a short period (ca. 1575 to 1598), and all we know about the author is what he provides in the work itself. He states that, prior to the

chronicle, he had composed five collections of poetry. Given this pronounced investment in the craft, it is perhaps not surprising that his use of
poetry in the chronicle makes a claim of uniqueness in a statement that
I translate in full:

> It should not remain hidden from the sound dispositions and upright minds of
> those who are aware of conventions of speech and are arrangers of gems in
> the manner of strings of pearls that the author of this text, the producer of
> these marks of black ink, has adhered to two propitious matters in putting
> together this work that are unprecedented among those dedicated to the
> chronicler's craft, past or present.
>
> The first of these is that he has not utilized verses of anyone other than
> himself while composing this book. Wherever there was a need for employ-
> ing verse for the sake of elegance and beauty, he has not deployed even
> a single verse save for one couplet from Amir Khosrow's *Ā'eneh-ye
> Sekandari* (The Alexandrian Mirror) that is included in the preface due to
> its eminent suitability for the purpose.
>
> The second matter is that he has abstained from mixing meters [*bohur*],
> deeming it imperative that wherever there is verse, it is in one particular
> meter, save for three quatrains to be found in the book's introduction.
> Consequently, if all the verses to be found in the book were to be extracted
> and put together sequentially, the collection would form a separate book unto
> itself. This meter is *motaqāreb ghayr sālem, maqsur*, or *mahzuf*. It has a five-
> fold structure, three voweled [*motaharrek*] and two unvoweled [*sāken*] feet,
> and the rhythm [*vazn*] of each half-verse is according to the scansion three
> *fa'ulon* and one *fa'ul*, with the *lām* of *fa'ul* at rest.
>
> This is the rhythm of Ferdowsi's *Shāhnāmeh*, Nezāmi's *Sekandarnāmeh*,
> Sa'di's *Bostān*, Khosrow Dehlavi's *Ā'eneh-ye Sekandari*, Jāmi's *Kheradnāmeh*,
> Khwāju-ye Kermāni's *Homāy va Homāyun*, Salmān Sāvaji's *Ferāqnāmeh*, and
> the *Temurnāmeh* of Hātefi, the second Ferdowsi. Numerous other masters of
> speech and eloquent poets have also composed many pearl-scattering *masnavis*
> in this meter and rhythm. (10–11)

As I indicated earlier in the discussion of Khwāfi's translation, the use of
poetry in the chronicle genre is quite normative. By the sixteenth century,
a work that did not incorporate poetic citations may even have been seen as
inadequately articulate. However, Natanzi's work is exceptional for two
reasons. The first has to do with the way he is bringing the Persian poetic
tradition into his work. Normally, this is done through citing the work of earlier
poets mixed in with one's own compositions. Among other things, this is a way
for authors to showcase their deep learning.

Natanzi was clearly intimately familiar with the tradition, as evident from the
list of earlier works he provides. But what he is citing from these works is the
meter rather than the words. The choice reflects the conceit that he can compose

as well as these earlier authorities. Emulating the form is the homage to a long-standing tradition, in that the earlier poets also seem to have "echoed" each other through the adoption of a certain rhythm in language. The innovation here is to name the pattern as a concern of history and then embed it within the surrounding prose form of the chronicle.

The second notable claim put forth by Natanzi is that, if all the poetry to be found in the work were assembled in a series, it would form a single poem. This is not difficult to do in the technical sense, since *masnavi* is a form of narrative poetry in which the rhyme changes with each couplet while maintaining the same meter and rhythm. *Masnavis* that have tens of thousands of verses are common. But Natanzi's claim is that he has written two works: the prosimetrical chronicle that anyone can read; and a long poem that has been braided into the prose.

It is one thing to encounter the poetry in the flow of the prose and quite another to take the poetry out and reassemble it into a single poem. In the first instance, the verses' meaning comes from the prose context in which they occur. In the second, verses before and after provide the context, potentially transforming their meanings completely. By inviting the reader to think of the verses as a single poem, Natanzi imbues his work with mystery and the potential to have hidden messages. One may read this to imply that the prosimetric text is for the ordinary reader while the text revealed by putting the verses together has a hidden meaning meant for those willing to do the reassembly. Poetry then holds a key to his intended meaning that would not be evident to someone who had not read the work's introduction and then taken the trouble to rework the text. The subliminal possibility incorporates subversiveness within the text, which the author may use to evade political supervision from his patrons and others in power.

For present purposes, the important thing about Natanzi's claim is that it shows us an especially complex way to instrumentalize poetry in the domain of history. Extracting poetry from the text and then seeing what it means on its own when serialized is quite difficult, since every instance of a jump between two poetic utterances requires the reader to rethink the meanings entirely. I have found that to provide even a single example of the changes that happen is beyond the space available to me in this Element. This is because all the poetic utterances require explanation when translated into English by themselves. Then to show the difference when the prose before and after them is replaced by earlier and later poetic insertions makes matters exponentially more complex. The intricacy of this proposition is overwhelming even when no translation is involved. The key thing, then, is Natanzi's claim regarding what he is doing rather than an assessment of how he implements it. On that score, the example gives a maximal sense for how poetry affected historiography in the Persian world. The kind of intricacy Natanzi is putting into operation for history can be found instantiated in almost all other domains of literary activity in the Persian world under consideration.

4.3 Memoir

Zaynoddin Vāsefi's *Badāye'-ol-vaqāye'* is an extraordinary memoir of Herat, penned in Tashkent (Uzbekistan) circa 1538–9, during the author's exile from his homeland following the Safavid takeover of the city in 1512. The narrative is an extended series of vignettes in which the author relates to his Central Asian audience his memories of encounters from his early life in Herat in the company of poets and other members of the court of the legendary Timurid monarch Hosayn Bāyqarā mentioned earlier.

The city, as it appears in these vignettes, is primarily the setting for encounters, gatherings, and competitions whose liveliness is conveyed through poetic citations. The work is an intimate, first-person account that is also utterly filled with generic conventions pertaining to Persian poetry. It provides one of the richest views of a great Persian city whose working fuel was poetic invention.

The work is, on one hand, a representation of the poetic "landscape" of the times; on the other, it is in itself an operationalization of common poetic tropes that subsume the city's physical and social characteristics. The work's play on relationships between memory, imagination, and experience is comparable to that of famous narratives such as Marcel Proust's *In Search of Lost Time* and James Joyce's *Ulysses*. However, here the foremost vehicle and paradigm for literary expression is poetry rather than prose. A reading of Vāsefi's work focused on rhetorical construction furthers our understanding of the social role of poetry in the Persian world.

Vāsefi begins with a vivid account of his personal experience of the capture of Herat by Shāh Esmaʻil in 1512. Since he identified with the vanquished party, this event compelled Vāsefi to go into self-imposed exile in Central Asia, where he served various Uzbek courts in the capacity of poet and boon companion to royalty. As he describes it himself, his patrons valued him particularly because of his status as a raconteur about Bāyqarā's court.

Vāsefi's narrative moves back and forth between various times in a complex way. The beginning connects his point of writing (1539) to the pivotal moment in his own life when Herat was captured (1512). Subsequently, all the information he provides is couched in the form of relating a personal experience or his response to his patrons when they ask about people or events concerned with Bāyqarā's court. As a result, the frames for the vignettes are all placed between the years 1512 and 1539, whereas the stories themselves belong almost entirely to the period before 1512. This pattern imbues the work with a thoroughly nostalgic mood in which the reader is invited into the narrative at one point and then swiftly transported to earlier times that come across as having been filled with greater adventure.

The overall quality of Vāsefi's play on time is best explained through examples. In the beginning of the work, Vāsefi tells that he had come to the point of denouncing the conquerors in public and thereby courting instant death. While on his way to do this, he came across an acquaintance who suggested that, instead, he should visit a man with the sobriquet Abol-jud (Father of Generosity) who had arrived recently from Spain and possessed miraculous powers to set his devotees' minds at ease through his possession of sciences such as alchemy, gematria, mathematics, and various forms of magic. This led to an encounter in which Abol-jud gave Vāsefi a highly detailed account of his future, telling that he would migrate to Central Asia, serve particular kings and princes descended from Genghis Khan, and eventually write a work entitled *Badāye'-ol-vaqāye'*. Overcome by this information, Vāsefi fainted in the man's company and then never saw him again. However, the prognostication he had provided soon began to come true when he availed himself of the opportunity to join a caravan going toward Central Asia (1:5–8).

Vāsefi left Herat for Central Asia in 1512 in the company of associates who either knew one another already or became friends in the midst of their common affliction. Those present in the party were bound for two different destinations, which compelled the group to break into two at a river crossing. Some companions decided to commemorate this event with verses. The first offered the following quatrain:

> Like the Pleiades, in a moment, we had come together,
>> the way jewels become sewn side by side in a garment.
> All of a sudden, heaven split the thread of that union,
>> flinging each piece away to a different corner of the world.

To this, a second responded with a short poem (*qet'eh*):

> In this disappointing abode,
>> better not to become attached to someone.
> For everyone on whom you may set your heart,
>> his hypocritical company will be spiritual torture,
>> if his demeanor is anathema to your nature.
> And if his manners accord well with your ways,
>> separating from him will give the taste of death's elixir.

And finally, Vāsefi himself provided a short poem:

> When gathered letters, joined one to other, mark company full of pleasures,
>   the heavenly sphere takes up enmity and the will to quarrel.
> Casting a thousand tricks and subterfuges in the way,
>   it causes separation, as manifest in the letters of farewell.

(1:35)

Vāsefi's contribution here contains a play on the way the words "gathered" (*jam'*) and "farewell" (*vedā'*) are written in the Arabic script: the first contains letters that are joined when they are written together, whereas the second contains letters that must be written separately.

As portrayed in these verses, human life appears suspended between individuals' volition and desire to be together, on the one hand, and the disruptive play of heavenly powers, on the other. The ultimate marker of togetherness is discourse, celebrated most prominently through the act of poetic invention. The heavens move on in their regularity, going about the business of influencing human lives without care for individual fortunes, while the human experience is conditioned fundamentally by the pains and pleasures of communal interactions.

A later section of the work is entitled "On this poor wretch's losing his heart to the goblet of love of Maqsud-e Khammār." Here Vāsefi provides the story of an amorous encounter he had while living in Samarkand (1:138–162). The object of love here is Maqsud-e Khammār, a phrase that is the personal name of a man but can also be read as both the "desired winemaker" and "desired intoxication." Some details of this account will help to demonstrate the interplay between the conduct of life and poetic metaphors and performances as comes across in Vāsefi's narrative.

He states that one day when he was in a shop in the perfumers' bazaar of Samarkand talking about poetry, there was suddenly a huge commotion. The shop owner said that this must be because of Maqsud-e Khammār, a beautiful young man of the city. Hearing of this, the company began reciting verses regarding his beauty, beginning with his exquisite stature.

The man eventually became visible and when Vāsefi's eyes landed on his face, he was entranced by a mole in between his eyebrows and invented a verse about it. The company then went around, some composing and other reciting existing verses on the man's eyebrows, downy cheeks, mole, black hair, forelock, mouth, and nose. When the man suddenly left, Vāsefi realized that he had fallen in love with him and felt utterly bereft (1:139–142).

Vāsefi then went looking for him, and some people told him that the man was originally from Shahrisabz (Uzbekistan) and had come to Samarkand and opened a wineshop by the white bridge. Then they complained:

Everyone in the world seems to be headed there. If that mischievous disturber of city's peace [*shahrāshub*] continues in this way, nothing of asceticism, goodness, and well-being will remain. Ascetics and worshippers will pledge their cloaks and prayer rugs for wine. Distinguished scholars will utterly forget their books of sacred law:

> When such are the eye, eyebrow, elegance, and flirting,
>> adieu knowledge and wisdom, goodbye intellect and faith.
>>>> *(1:143)*

Hearing this, Vāsefi too headed to the bridge. All the city's grandees were there, crowding in the wineshop as Maqsud stood in a black loincloth and rosy hat, straining wine. He welcomed Vāsefi and asked his name. He replied with a verse:

> Since this slave describes beautiful people,
>> he has become famous as the describer [*vāsefi*].
>>>> *(1:144)*

Maqsud took a liking to Vāsefi, and they met alone near a pond where Vāsefi said a verse in his praise:

> All our life we ran around the streets purposeless [*bi-maqsud*].
>> In tavern's alley we reached the purpose [*maqsud*].

Maqsud liked the verse and suggested that there be a gathering at the wine-shop, since all the city's great people were already present there. Maqsud introduced Vāsefi, praised the verse he had said, and indicated that an earlier acquaintance had told him that Vāsefi had had great adventures during his life in Herat. Vāsefi was then invited to share the stories, which he proceeded to do in detail, liberally interlaced with his own poetry, verses from companions he had known in Herat, and citations from earlier great poets (1:145).

When Vāsefi was done with one long story, involving 'Alishir Navā'i and Jāmi among others, Maqsud suggested another one, which got him going again (1:155). When this was done, Maqsud stood up to say that what he had heard had compelled him to change his ways. He now wanted nothing more than to become a religious student. He took up instruction from Vāsefi and was transformed from a corrupting beloved to a righteous person (1:162).

Vāsefi's account of Maqsud-e Khammār begins with disorder and ends with order. This is a pattern deployed dozens of time in the long work. The dichotomy maps closely to poetry versus prose: people start speaking verses as soon as Maqsud-e Khammār's presence is felt, and the passion unleashed onto the city by him is gradually brought to heel by Vāsefi narrating stories from his past. While order wins out on the surface in the end, poetry is the undercurrent that drives the narrative throughout.

The brief description of Vāsefi's work I have provided is an exceedingly poor reflection of the original text. Virtually every sentence and verse of the original is filled with allusions and double meanings. Moreover, the boundary between fact and fiction in this work is, by design, entirely unclear. The author's purpose is to translate the set fictional scene of the poetic dialect into life stories with himself as the central character. This is amply evident in the story of Maqsud. A devastatingly handsome wine seller, whose body is metonymic to his wares, is a common poetic trope. Maqsud's effort to engage Vāsefi in telling stories puts him in the same position as a confidant who sells wine and gets to hear lovers talk. Throughout the rest of the narrative as well, tropes are constantly put into lifelike situations, whereas whatever is observed about people and events is made metaphorical or poetic through inserting verses. The result is a work that, to the knowing reader, feels like becoming privy to Persian poetry's inside story. For someone who would not know the allusions and references, it may come across as overly ornate and trivial.

4.4 Collections

Some of the most intriguing yet enigmatic sources available for the study of Persian poetry as a social concern are collections made over the course of centuries. These are "complex instruments," about which we can say for sure that they were valuable to those who created and preserved them. They contain excerpts of all manner, ranging from snippets of the works of famous poets to those of others about whom nothing is known save for the bit to be found in the collections. Despite the fact that we know them to be important for social history, these works are difficult to interpret because they do not come with a narrative that would explain the impetus for creation. Academic work on such collections has been progressing slowly, led by experts who specialize in various regions and periods pertaining to the Persian world (e.g. Afshar, 2011; Babayan, 2021). To provide a concrete sense for this material, I will briefly describe three collections that are remarkable for different reasons.

4.4.1 Shams Hāji's Ship

The first collection I consider has the completion date of Rajab 741 (December 1340–January 1341) and has been edited and published recently under the title *Safineh-ye Shams Hāji* (Shams Hāji's Ship). All that is known about the compiler is his name, Shams Hāji Shirāzi, and that he was alive as late as 1354, the year given on another manuscript for which he was the copyist (39). While the name implies origins in Shiraz, a poem of his own included in the collection contains praise for the Golden Horde ruler Jāni Bayg Khān (d. 1357).

Other indications found in the manuscript suggest that his literary life was divided among Inner Asia, Crimea, Anatolia, and Azerbaijan (39–45).

To refer to collections of poetry and other excerpts as boats filled with bits and pieces has a long history. This explains the use of terms such as *safineh* and *jong* for them, the latter term having a Chinese origin that is shared with the English word "junk." The list of contents of Shams Hāji's ship shows it to be a snapshot of the tradition of Persian poetry refracted through the taste of the compiler. It contains selections from fifty-nine named poets (fifty-eight men and one woman) and sixty-six verses that are anonymous. The most quoted poet is Sa'di (1,185 verses), followed by the compiler himself (544 verses) and numerous others among the famous (such as Rumi, Sanā'i, and 'Attār), as well as ones whom we know only from the mention in this collection (55–57). The compiler's self-citations indicate that he saw himself as a practitioner of the poetic art and not just as a compiler. His own work is learned and competent, although without the kind of ingenuity that would have made him a reference point for those writing after him (536–553). The following quatrain is a sample:

> Suddenly, we have become servant to worshippers of wine.
> We have become drunk from the season's last draught.
> We were parrot and then became a nightingale.
> Being nightingale, we have turned into a thousand tales.
>
> *(553)*

This collection is comparable to numerous other that survive (93–114), providing evidence that curating poetry was a pastime with a wide footprint in society. The fact that personal choices went into collecting is evident from observations such as the fact that Shams Hāji's work does not have a single verse from the most famous Persian poetic work of all time, Ferdowsi's *Shāhnāmeh*. Assessing details of issues such as this choice gets us to subjective postures projected within an overall deep investment in the tradition as a whole.

4.4.2 An Anthology Preserved in South India

The second collection I introduce is different from that of Shams Hāji on account of containing famous poetry only, copied in an expert hand, accompanied by miniature paintings of a very high quality. Now at the Chester Beatty Library in Dublin, this two-volume work has 1435–6 as the year of copying (Arberry, Minovi, and Blochet, 1959: 1:45–53). Of the two named copyists, one has a name indicating a suburb in Isfahan, although the collection does not give the place of manufacture itself. The manuscripts do, however, have a seal of ownership. A note states that, in 1514, the collection was purchased for inclusion in the library of Soltān Esmāʻil ʻĀdelshāh of Bijapur (Karnataka, India). The work's presence in South India reflects the high level of investment in Persian literature and culture in South India in the fifteenth and sixteenth centuries (Flatt, 2019).

This collection contains the works of Nezāmi, Rumi, Amir Khosrow, Busiri (translated from Arabic), ʻAttār, and Saʻdi. While we do not know the circumstances of commission, the quality of calligraphy and paintings suggests a royal patron, whether ʻĀdelshāh himself or someone else from whom the collection was acquired for the royal library in South India. Each page of the anthology has two texts: one in the center and another on the margins. In the example I have chosen for illustration (see Figure 9), the central text is Nezāmi's *Eskandarnāmeh* (Book of Alexander), while the margins have Rumi's *Masnavi*. The painting in this instance is showing Alexander's funeral procession. The two volumes of the anthology together consist of 597 folios, with a total of 121 finely executed paintings. These statistics make this collection one of the most elaborate manuscripts of classics of Persian poetry surviving from the Middle Ages.

On the surface of it, this anthology may be seen as a straightforward collection of some classics of Persian poetry. However, I regard it as a complex poetic instrument because the manuscript that contains the text signifies the work of poets, critics, calligraphers, painters, and wealthy consumers. Varied interests and desires of these groups caused the manuscript to be created and bought and sold across Iran and India. The history of this artifact therefore encompasses far more than the poetic text we can read in any number of different places. It reflects the socioeconomic situation as a whole centered on the value of extraordinary Persian poetry.

4.4.3 Golshan Album

The last collection I will highlight here is known as the Golshan Album, put together between 1600 and 1618 for the Mughal king Jahāngir in North India. This work straddles the period when Jahāngir was first a crown prince with a separate court and then became the emperor in 1605. The history of the Golshan Album after its removal from the Mughal royal library is unclear. At some point, a majority of it ended up in the Qajar court in Iran, where it can be located in the nineteenth century in the library of the Golestan Palace (Beach, 2013; Safarzadeh, 2011). Many leaves from the original album were dispersed and have ended up in libraries and museums around the world. I would like to draw attention to a single leaf from the Golshan Album, now at the Chester Beatty Library, Dublin (see Figure 10) (Leach, 1995; Wright, 2008). The

Figure 9 Alexander's funeral procession from a copy of Nezāmi's *Eskandarnāmeh*, an anthology of Persian poetry. Copied by ʿAli Pagir al-Ashtarjāni, 1435. Paper, pigment, ink, and gold: 39.2 × 26.7 cm. © The Trustees of the Chester Beatty Library, Dublin. MS Per 1241, Folio 299a.

elegance and complexity of this one page, assembled in the early seventeenth century, allows a summation of the tradition whose story I have attempted to tell in this Element.

Figure 10 A folio from the Gulshan Album. India, 1600–1618, with elements from Iran and Nuremberg. Paper, pigment, ink, and gold: 41 × 25.5 cm. © The Trustees of the Chester Beatty Library, Dublin. In 47.12.

The page shown in Figure 10 is a composite on multiple levels. It contains a mixture of text and images, which went together in the context of works produced for the Mughal court (Rice, 2014). Human figures, animals, and mythical beings occupy various places. The background consists of a mixture of nature and highly stylized geometric patterns in multiple colors. And the materials we see have Indian, Iranian, and European origins.

For my purposes, the best place to begin is the single line of Persian text. This comes from Sa'di, a master poet whom I have mentioned multiple times in this Element. What is being quoted here is a snippet from the prose part of a story in Sa'di's prosimetric work *Golestān* (Rose Garden). The text is not readily understandable, in that it says the following: "give and do not bring such violence upon him that on the day of resurrection than you." To understand this text requires that one knows Sa'di's original, where the story goes as follows (I have put the text on the Golshan Album page in italics):

A pious man passed by someone on whom God had bestowed bounty, who had tied up a slave and was berating him. He said, "Son, since God, exalted and glorified, has bound another creature under your control, he has given you precedence over him. *Give* thanks to God *and do not bring such violence upon him that on the day of resurrection*, he looks better *than you* and causes you to be shameful:

Do not berate the slave.
Do not torture him, nor sadden his heart.
You have just purchased him with ten dirhams.
You are not the one who created him with your power.
How long will this rule, arrogance, and domination go on?
There is a lord greater than you as well.
Owner of Arslān and Āghush,
do not forget the one who issues commands to you.

(Sa'di, 1964: 169)

While the text on the album page may seem random, it reflects the fact that, in context, most people who would have reason to see the page would have readily identified the text from memory. Sa'di's works were part of the curriculum for inculcating literacy and refined behavior from childhood onward in the Persian world. This particular story contains a moral lesson addressed to the powerful, something quite apt to go into a collection meant for the self-cultivation of a prince or king. Such exhortation is a general feature of the material in the Golshan Album and similar works (Koch, 2011).

What we see on the Golshan Album page is, literally, an intertext, whose significance requires knowing the larger tradition. In the Persian poetic tradition, a verse occupied a similar position in that it called out to conventions and precedents. To understand and evaluate the wares in this context required knowing the larger market in which they traded.

The relationship between the text and the images is not entirely clear here. Backgrounds of various types fill the page, the gold highlighting giving everything a glowing appearance. The birds and the lion are cited from a long history in this type of miniature painting. While the borders are Indian, the human figures are of Iranian origin. The largest person bears the signature *mashq-e Rezā*, meaning it claims to be the work of the very famous Iranian Safavid artist Rezā-ye 'Abbāsi (d. 1635). The presence of these images, pasted on paper, references the long history of poetic and other transferences between Iran and India.

For someone used to looking at Persian miniature paintings, the most unusual element on this page is the European engraving located in the top left quadrant. As in the case of the Iranian drawings, this is a pre-made element incorporated into the composition. Produced between 1530 and 1562 in Nuremberg, Germany, by Virgil Solis, the image shows the moon (luna) "riding a chariot drawn by dolphins to right; holding a crescent moon in her left hand; below fishermen and a mill at right; from a series of seven engravings of planetary gods riding chariots with signs of the Zodiac represented on the wheels" (British Museum, 1869, 0410.181; Peters, 1987: 83). Jahāngir is known to have been interested in European Christianity, and there are numerous other cases of such incorporation of European figural elements in the Golshan Album and associated objects (Beach, 1965).

This page from the Gulshan Album has an aesthetic unity that belies the disparate origins of the elements that went into creating it. What we see here is a reflection of the courtly world of India in the early seventeenth century, where people and objects from all over came into contact. It seems to me that we can see this composite, intertextual, and inter-image page as emblematic of what I have tried to describe in this Element. Poetry in the Persian world during the Middle Ages constituted a recognizable market of exchange going across times and spaces. It was, however, never insular or entirely bounded. It is best seen as an arena, transforming and transformational, that affected the lives of millions of people over centuries.

Conclusion

By thematizing Persian poetry as a ware enmeshed in market relations in this Element, my hope has been to highlight its role as a crucially important element for producing, preserving, and communicating ideas and practices over times and spaces. In this sense, Persian poetry is a global phenomenon spanning worlds past and present.

My discussion can be recapped by pointing to three issues that have come up in various places. First, evolving over a millennium, Persian poetry was a multigenre discursive realm that operated based on tacit rules of engagement. Poetic production was iterative, requiring practitioners to learn the tradition's implicit standards from earlier work and to position their own compositions relative to those of their predecessors and contemporaries. Discussions regarding valuation ran concurrently with the creation of poetry, reflecting an art form whose proponents were self-conscious about its aims and social value.

Second, seen societally, poetry came about through a mixture of consensus and contestation among the people who composed, patronized, and traded it. This means that poetic products bore a close relationship to the social status of all participants in the market, including matters pertaining to class, regional affiliation, and gender. Despite Persian poetry's highly formalized rules, its contents, as well as information about the lives of poets, provide us extensive access to power relations prevalent in the societies where it held sway. On this score, we cannot take discourse about poetry at face value and must interpret it in light of our knowledge of poetic conventions.

Third, Persian poetry was fundamentally an aesthetic matter, inseparable from valuation pertaining to pleasure, emotions, and ethics. Observing variation of poetic taste across time and space illuminates literary and cultural life across Eurasia. Poetic practice in Persian generated distinctive encasements for expressing universal human concerns. For adept creators, listeners, and readers, the ability to engage poetic expression permeated subjectivity to the point of becoming an instinct.

Of the three factors I have enumerated, the aesthetic dimension of Persian poetry from the Middle Ages has continued to hold immense value in modern times. Poetry of the past, and new poetry written in imitation of past idioms, looms large in civic and literary life in societies where Persian remains a major literary vehicle. Importantly, the valuation on this score is spread across a spectrum. It includes poetry being seen as both a great inheritance from the past and a mark of decadence that must be overcome in order for societies to become dynamic and properly modern (Ahmadi, 2008; Karim-Hakkak, 1995; Khalid, 2015: 291–295, 305–315; Najafian, 2018).

My discussion in Section 4 of this Element ended on a work where a European artifact (Virgil Solis's Luna) is found on an object created in the seventeenth century in the Persian world (a page of the Golshan Album). The other side of this coin is that Persian ideas and materials have been flowing to Europe for centuries as well. Persian poetry has had a surprisingly robust place in Euro-American thought and literature, especially since the eighteenth century. This interest is keyed to aesthetic factors involving the idiom's suitability for expressing modern existential concerns.

Once introduced to poets such as Hāfez, European intellectuals such as Johann Wolfgang von Goethe (d. 1832) became invested in a kind of Persophilia (Dabashi, 2015). Commercially, the most successful book of English poetry in the nineteenth century was Edward FitzGerald's translations of the Persian quatrains of 'Omar Khayyām (d. 1131) (Khayyam, 1997; Richardson, 2016). More recently in the English world in particular, translations of the Persian poetry of Jalāloddin Rumi have been among the biggest sellers in the poetry market (Azadbougar and Patton, 2015; Lewis, 2000: 499–527). As reflected in the names and nationalities of scholars I have cited, Persian poetry has been a preoccupation for scholars working in all European languages that have significant scholarly literatures. As a work written for readers of English, this Element, too, is a part of Persian poetry's reach extending over times, places, and languages.

To note the traffic in poetry within and beyond the Persian world is to register the permeability of temporal and spatial boundaries pertaining to the Middle Ages. The Persian world I have tried to illuminate is an abstraction that was, in historical terms, always in the making. It existed, and continues to exist, enmeshed with other linguistic and cultural worlds, including those of Europe. Similarly, the Middle Ages are a modern object, made up in hindsight, by peoples seeking to understand change keyed to time. As a narrative of the story of Persian poetry, this Element has presented the world as made available in materials created in the Middle Ages, while remaining cognizant of conceptual commitments that pertain to us as twenty-first-century interpreters.

References

Afshar, I. (2011). *Safineh va bayāz va jong: Maqāleh-hā-ye Iraj-e Afshār*. Tehran: Sokhan.

Ahmadi, W. (2008). *Modern Persian Literature in Afghanistan: Anomalous Visions of History and Form*. London: Routledge.

Allsen, T. T. (2019). *The Steppe and the Sea: Pearls in the Mongol Empire*. Philadelphia: University of Pennsylvania Press.

Amanat, A., and Ashraf, A., eds. (2018). *The Persianate World: Rethinking a Shared Sphere*. Leiden: Brill.

Ambraseys, N. N., and C. P. Melville. (1982). *A History of Persian Earthquakes*. Cambridge: Cambridge University Press.

Arberry, A. J., Minovi, M., and Blochet, E. (1959). *The Chester Beatty Library: A Catalogue of the Persian Manuscripts and Miniatures*. 3 vols. Dublin: Hodges, Figgis and Co Ltd.

'Aruzi, A. N. (1910). *Chahār maqāleh*, ed. Mirzā Mohammad Qazwini. Leiden: Brill.

Awhadi-Balyāni, T. (2010). *'Arafātol-'āsheqin va 'arasātol-'ārefin*, ed. Z. Sāhibkāri, A. F. Ahmad, and M. Qahrmān, 8 vols. Tehran: Mirās-e Maktub.

'Awfi, M. (1906). *Lobābol-albāb*, ed. E. G. Browne, 2 vols. Leiden: Brill.

Azadibougar, O., and Patton, S. (2015). Coleman Barks' Versions of Rumi in the USA. *Translation and Literature* **24**(2), 172–189.

Babayan, K. (2021). *The City as Anthology: Eroticism and Urbanity in Early Modern Isfahan*. Stanford, CA: Stanford University Press.

Bābor, Z. (1995). *Bābornāmeh: Vaqāye'*, ed. Eiji Mano, 2 vols. Kyoto: Syokado.

Bashir, S. (2011). *Sufi Bodies: Religion and Society in Medieval Islam*. New York: Columbia University Press.

Bashir, S. (Forthcoming, 2022). *A New Vision for Islamic Pasts and Futures*. Cambridge, MA: MIT Press.

Beach, M. C. (1965). The Gulshan Album and Its European Sources. *Bulletin of the Museum of Fine Arts* **63**(332), 63–91.

Beach, M. C. (2013). The Gulshan Album and the Workshops of Prince Salim. *Artibus Asiae* **73**(2), 445–477.

Beelaert, A. L. (2019). Recent Work on Classical Persian Literature: A Wake-up Call. *Asiatische Studien – Études Asiatiques* **73**(4), 889–917.

Beers, T. (2015). The Biography of Vahshi Bāfqi (d. 991/1583) and the Tazkera Tradition. *Journal of Persianate Studies* **8**, 195–222.

Bernardini, M. (2003). Hātifi's Timurnāmeh and Qāsimi's Shāhnāmeh-yi Ismāʿil: Considerations for a Double Critical Edition. In A. J. Newman, ed., *Society and Culture in the Early Modern Middle East: Studies on Iran in the Safavid Period*, pp. 3–18. Leiden: Brill.

Black, J. (2018). *Geographies of An Imperial Power: The British World, 1688–1815*. Bloomington: Indiana University Press.

Brookshaw, D. P. (2019). *Hafiz and His Contemporaries: Poetry, Performance and Patronage in Fourteenth-Century Iran*. London: I. B. Tauris.

Burgel, J.- C., and Van Ruymbeke, C. (2011). *A Key to the Treasure of the Hakim: Artistic and Humanistic Aspects of Nizāmi Ganjavi's Khamsa*. Leiden: Leiden University Press.

Csirkés, F. (2019). A Messiah Untamed: Notes on the Philology of Shah Ismāʿil's Divān. *Iranian Studies* **52**(3–4), 339–395.

Dabashi, H. (2015). *Persophilia: Persian Culture on the Global Scene*. Cambridge, MA: Harvard University Press.

Dale, S. F. (2004). *The Garden of the Eight Paradises: Bābur and the Culture of Empire in Central Asia, Afghanistan and India (1483–1530)*. Leiden: Brill.

Davidson, O. M. (2013). *Poet and Hero in the Persian Book of Kings*, 3rd edn. Boston, MA: Ilex Foundation.

Davis, D. (1999). Sufism and Poetry: A Marriage of Convenience? *Edebiyât* **10**(2), 279–292.

de Bruijn, J. T. P. (1997). *Persian Sufi Poetry: An Introduction to the Mystical Use of Classical Persian Poems*. Richmond, Surrey: Curzon.

de la Cadena, M., and Blaser, M. (2018). *A World of Many Worlds*. Durham, NC: Duke University Press.

d'Hubert, T. and Papas, A., eds. (2019). *Jāmi in Regional Contexts: The Reception of ʿAbd al-Rahmān Jāmi's Works in the Islamicate World, ca. 9th/15th–14th/20th Century*. Leiden: Brill.

Ebn-e Monavvar, M. (2003). *Asrār at-tawhid fi maqāmāt ash-Shaykh Abi Saʿid*, ed. M. Shafiʿi-Kadkani, 2 vols. Tehran: Muʾassaseh-ye Enteshārāt-e Āgāh.

Fakhri-Heravi, S. M. (1968). *Tazkereh-ye rawzāt as-salātin va Javāher al-ʿajāʾeb, maʿ Divān-e Fakhri-Heravi*, ed. P. H. Rāshedi. Hyderabad, Pakistan: Sindhi Adabi Board.

Flatt, E. J. (2019). *The Courts of the Deccan Sultanates: Living Well in the Persian Cosmopolis*. Cambridge: Cambridge University Press.

Gallagher, A. (2018). The Apocalypse of Ecstasy: The Poetry of Shah Ismāʿil Revisited. *Iranian Studies* **51**(3), 361–397.

Golchin-Maʿāni, A. (1984). *Tārikh-e tazkereh'hā-ye Fārsi*, 2 vols. Tehran: Enteshārāt-e Ketābkhāneh-ye Sanāʾi.

Green, N. (2019). *The Persianate World*. Oakland: University of California Press.

Haeri, Niloofar. (2021). *Say What Your Longing Heart Desires: Women, Prayer, and Poetry in Iran*. Stanford, CA: Stanford University Press.

Ingenito, D. (2018). Hafez's "Shirāzi Turk": A Geopoetical Approach. *Iranian Studies* **51**(6), 851–887.

Karimi-Hakkak, A. (1995). *Recasting Persian Poetry: Scenarios of Poetic Modernity in Iran*. Salt Lake City: University of Utah Press.

Keshavarz, F. (1998). *Reading Mystical Lyric: The Case of Jalal al-Din Rumi*. Columbia: University of South Carolina Press.

Keshavmurthy, P. (2011). Finitude and the Authorship of Fiction: Muhammad 'Awfi's Preface to his Chronicle, *Lubāb al-albāb* (The Piths of Intellects). *Arab Studies Journal* **19**(1), 94–120.

Khalid, A. (2015). *Making Uzbekistan*. Ithaca, NY: Cornell University Press.

Khayyam, O. (1997). *Edward FitzGerald, Rubáiyát of Omar Khayyám: A Critical Edition*. Charlottesville: University Press of Virginia.

Khwāfi, Z. K. (n.d.). *Tabaqāt-e Bābori*, MS. Or. 1999, British Library, London.

Kinra, R. (2015). *Writing Self, Writing Empire: Chandar Bhan Brahman and the Cultural World of the Indo-Persian State Secretary*. Oakland: University of California Press.

Koch, E. (2011). The Mughal Emperor as Solomon, Majnun, and Orpheus, Or the Album as a Think Tank for Allegory. *Muqarnas* **27**, 277–312.

Landau, A. (2015). *Pearls on a String: Artists, Patrons, and Poets at the Great Islamic Courts*. Seattle: University of Washington Press.

Landau, J. (2013). *De rythme et de raison: Lecture croisée de deux traités de poétique persans du XViiie siècle*. Paris: Presses Sorbonne Nouvelle.

Leach, L. Y. (1995). *Mughal and Other Indian Paintings from the Chester Beatty Library*. London: Scorpion Cavendish.

Lewis, F. (1994). The Rise and Fall of a Persian Refrain. In S. Stetkevych, ed., *Reorientations: Arabic and Persian Poetry*, pp. 199–226. Bloomington: Indiana University Press.

Lewis, F. (2000). *Rumi: Past and Present, East and West*. Oxford: Oneworld.

Lewis, F. (2019). To Round and Rondeau the Canon: Jāmī and Fānī's Reception of the Persian Lyrical Tradition. In T. d'Hubert and A. Papas, eds., *Jāmi in Regional Contexts: The Reception of 'Abd al-Rahmān Jāmi's Works in the Islamicate World, ca. 9th/15th–14th/20th Century*, pp. 463–567. Leiden: Brill.

Losensky, P. E. (1998a). Linguistic and Rhetorical Aspects of the Signature Verse (*Takhallus*) in the Persian Ghazal. *Edebiyât* **8**(2), 239–271.

Losensky, P. E. (1998b). *Welcoming Fighāni: Imitation and Poetic Individuality in the Safavid-Mughal Ghazal*. Costa Mesa, CA: Mazda Publishers.

Losensky, P. E., and Sharma, S. (2011). *In the Bazaar of Love: The Selected Poetry of Amir Khusrau*. New Delhi: Penguin Books India.

Lotfollāh (2006). *Hālāt va sokhanān-e Shaykh Abu Sa'id Abi l-Khayr*, ed. M. Shafi'i-Kadkani. Tehran: Enteshārāt-e Sokhan.

Manz, B. F. (2007). *Power, Politics and Religion in Timurid Iran*. Cambridge: Cambridge University Press.

Meisami, J. S. (1987). *Medieval Persian Court Poetry*. Princeton, NJ: Princeton University Press.

Mignolo, W. (2000). *Local Histories/Global Designs*. Princeton, NJ: Princeton University Press.

Miller, D., ed. (2005). *Materiality*. Durham, NC: Duke University Press.

Najafian, A. (2018). Poetic Nation: Iranian Soul and Historical Continuity. PhD dissertation, Stanford University.

Natanzi, M. (1994). *Noqāvat al-āsār fi zekr al-akhyār*, ed. Ehsān Eshrāqi. Tehran: Sherkat-e Enteshārāt-e 'Elmi va Farhangi.

Navā'i, A. (1945). *Majāles an-nafā'es*, ed. 'Ali Asghar Hekmat. Tehran: Chāpkhāneh-ye Bānk-i Melli-ye Irān.

Olszewska, Z. (2015). *The Pearl of Dari: Poetry and Personhood Among Young Afghans in Iran*. Bloomington: Indiana University Press.

O'Malley, A. (2019). From Blessed Lips: The Textualization of Abu Sa'id's Dicta and Deeds. *Journal of Persianate Studies* **12**(1), 5–31.

Peters, J. S. (1987). *German Masters of the Sixteenth Century: Virgil Solis: Intaglio Prints and Woodcuts*. New York: Abaris Books.

Qāsemi Gonābādi (2008). *Shāh Esmā'il-nāmeh*, ed. Ja'far Shojā'i-kiyā. Tehran: Farhangestān-e Zabān va Adab-e Fārsi.

Rāmi, H. (1947). *Anisol-'oshshāq*, ed. 'A. Eqbāl. Tehran: Sherkat-e Sahāmi.

Rice, Y. (2014). Between the Brush and the Pen: On the Intertwined Histories of Mughal Painting and Calligraphy. In D. Roxburgh, ed., *Envisioning Islamic Art and Architecture: Essays in Honor of Renata Holod*, pp. 148–174. Leiden: Brill.

Richardson, R. D. (2016). *Nearer the Heart's Desire: Poets of the Rubaiyat*. New York: Bloomsbury.

Rubanovich, J. (2015). *Orality and Textuality in the Iranian World: Patterns of Interaction Across the Centuries*. Leiden: Brill.

Sa'di, M. (1964). *Golestān-e Sa'di*, ed. M. J. Mashkur. Tehran: Eqbāl.

Safarzadeh, N. (2011). The History of the Muraqqa'-i Gulshan. *Artibus Asiae* **71**(1), 163–172.

Safavi, S. M. (2005). *Tazkereh-ye tohfeh-ye Sāmi*, ed. R. Homāyunfarrokh. Tehran: Asātir.

Samarqandi, D. (2007). *Tazkeratosh-sho'arā*, ed. F. 'Alaqeh. Tehran: Pezhuheshgāh-e 'Olum-e Ensāni va Motāle'āt-e Farhangi.

Schimmel, A. (1992). *A Two-Colored Brocade: The Imagery of Persian Poetry*. Chapel Hill: University of North Carolina Press.

Schwartz, K. L. (2020). *Remapping Persian Literary History, 1700–1900*. Edinburgh: Edinburgh University Press.

Shams Hāji (2011). *Safineh-ye Shams Hāji*, ed. Milād 'Azimi. Tehran: Sokhan.

Shams-e Qays Rāzi (2010). *Mo'jam fi ma'āyir-e ash'ār-e 'Ajam*, ed. M. Qazvini, M. Razavi, and S. Shamisā. Tehran: 'Elm.

Sharlet, J. (2011). *Patronage and Poetry in the Islamic World: Social Mobility and Status in the Medieval Middle East and Central Asia*. London: I. B. Tauris.

Sharma, S. (2005). *Amir Khusraw: The Poet of Sufis and Sultans*. Oxford: Oneworld.

Sharma, S. (2017). *Mughal Arcadia: Persian Literature in an Indian Court*. Cambridge, MA: Harvard University Press.

Subtelny, M. E. (1986). A Taste for the Intricate: The Persian Poetry of the Late Timurid Period. *Zeitschrift der Deutschen Morgenländischen Gesellschaft* **136**, 56–79.

Tanaka, S. (2019). *History Without Chronology*. Amherst, MA: Lever Press.

Truschke, A. (2020). A Padshah Like Manu: Political Advice for Akbar in the Persian Mahābhārata. *Philological Encounters* **5**(2), 112–133.

Utas, B. (2008). "Genres" in Persian Literature 900–1900. In C. Jahani and D. Kargar, eds., *Manuscript, Text and Literature: Collected Essays on Middle and New Persian Texts*, pp. 219–261. Wiesbaden: Reichert.

Van den Berg, G. R. (2004). *Minstrel Poetry from the Pamir Mountains: A Study on the Songs and Poems of the Ismā'ilis of Tajik Badakhshan*. Wiesbaden: Reichert.

Vāsefi, Z. (1961). *Badāye'-ol-vaqāye'*, ed. A. Boldyrev, 2 vols. Tehran: Enteshārāt-e Bonyād-e Farhang-e Iran.

Windfuhr, G. (1990). "Spelling the Mystery of Time." *Journal of the American Oriental Society* 110, no. 3: 401–416.

Wright, E. (2008). *Muraqqa': Imperial Mughal Albums from the Chester Beatty Library, Dublin*. Alexandria, VA: Art Services International.

Zipoli, R. (1993). *The Technique of the Ǧawāb: Replies by Nawā'i to Hāfiz and Ǧāmi*. Venice: Cafoscarina.

Acknowledgments

Discussions in this Element privilege my readings of a handful of works from a vast archive. As a cultural historian, I consider this to be the optimal way to provide a flavor of the world I wish to describe rather than a survey claiming to encompass as much as possible. Persian poetry has been the subject of an extensive scholarly literature. Limitations on length restrict me to mere references to existing publications instead of engaging with arguments in detail. What I am able to offer here is, nevertheless, owed to what I have learned from reading widely across the work of colleagues who specialize in historical and literary study of the Persian world. I hope they will consider references to their work to be a form of acknowledgment and gratitude.

A part of the work presented in this Element was undertaken during sabbatical leave made possible by fellowships from the John Simon Guggenheim Memorial Foundation and the Stanford Humanities Center. I am greatly appreciative of this support. Conversations with colleagues and friends over many years have fed into the creation and revision of this work. I am especially grateful to Mariam Aboukathir, Tanvir Ahmed, Vincent Barletta, Dominic Brookshaw, Jessica Chen, Robert Crews, Tara Dhaliwal, Jamal Elias, Parwana Fayyaz, Niloofar Haeri, Farooq Hamid, Adeeb Khalid, Paul Losensky, Carolina Mendoza, Jeremy Mumford, Ahoo Najafian, Tara Nummedal, Sholeh Quinn, Amy Remensnyder, William Sherman, CJ Uy, and Lee Yearley. My sincerest thanks to the two anonymous reviewers for the Press whose suggestions were a great help for clarifying the presentation.

Cambridge Elements ≡

The Global Middle Ages

Geraldine Heng

University of Texas at Austin

Geraldine Heng is Perceval Professor of English and Comparative Literature at the University of Texas, Austin. She is the author of *The Invention of Race in the European Middle Ages* (2018) and *England and the Jews: How Religion and Violence Created the First Racial State in the West* (2018), both published by Cambridge, as well as *Empire of Magic: Medieval Romance and the Politics of Cultural Fantasy* (2003, Columbia). She is the editor of *Teaching the Global Middle Ages* (2022, MLA), coedits the University of Pennsylvania Press series, RaceB4Race: Critical Studies of the Premodern, and is working on a new book, Early Globalisms: The Interconnected World, 500–1500 CE. Originally from Singapore, Heng is a Fellow of the Medieval Academy of America, a member of the Medievalists of Color, and Founder and Co-director, with Susan Noakes, of the Global Middle Ages Project: www.globalmiddleages.org.

Susan Noakes

University of Minnesota Twin Cities

Susan Noakes is Professor and Chair of French and Italian at the University of Minnesota, Twin Cities. From 2002 to 2008 she was Director of the Center for Medieval Studies; she has also served as Director of Italian Studies, Director of the Center for Advanced Feminist Studies, and Associate Dean for Faculty in the College of Liberal Arts. Her publications include *The Comparative Perspective on Literature: Essays in Theory and Practice* (coedited with Clayton Koelb, Cornell, 1988) and *Timely Reading: Between Exegesis and Interpretation* (Cornell, 1988), along with many articles and critical editions in several areas of French, Italian, and neo-Latin Studies. She is the Founder and Co-director, with Geraldine Heng, of the Global Middle Ages Project: www.globalmiddleages.org.

About the Series

Elements in the Global Middle Ages is a series of concise studies that introduce researchers and instructors to an uncentered, interconnected world, c. 500–1500 CE. Individual Elements focus on the globe's geographic zones, its natural and built environments, and its cultures, societies, arts, technologies, peoples, ecosystems, and lifeworlds.

Cambridge Elements ☰

The Global Middle Ages

Elements in the Series

A full series listing is available at: www.cambridge.org/EGMA

Printed in the United States
by Baker & Taylor Publisher Services